BUILDING

— *an* —

EMPIRE

The Most Complete Blueprint to Building

a Massive Network Marketing Business

BRIAN CARRUTHERS

Published by Next Century Publishing

Edited by Paul Braoudakis
Cover artwork by Alexander Vulchev
Layout and design by Paul Braoudakis
Diagrams and illustrations by Mark Demel

www.buildinganempirebook.com
www.fostermentor.com

ISBN 978-162-903-0128
Printed in the United States of America.

NEXT CENTURY
PUBLISHING

DEDICATION

I want to dedicate this book to my before and after.

To my dad for his incredible example of work ethic and entrepreneurism, and to my mom for her selfless giving and support through my whole life.

I also dedicate this book to my next generation, my son Talan. I trust that you will be inspired by your dad to know that life has no limits, and that you accomplish your wildest dreams.

Speaking of Dedication, I hope to be as dedicated to my family and my team as my parents have been to me.

ACKNOWLEDGMENTS

I owe a lifetime of gratitude to so many people. First, to my mentors who invested their time and energy into me – thank you! I'm not sure if you expected that I would see this through and take my business this seriously. But I soaked in everything you were willing to pour out, and I hope that my success is an extension of your legacy.

Second, I give my most sincere praise and appreciation to the builders and leaders whom I have had the privilege to work with on my team. You trusted in me, you followed me, and you accepted my no-fluff style of coaching. I truly stand on the shoulders of great men and women.

Third, I may never meet some of my teachers — the authors of books I read that shaped me. It's the people we meet and the books we read that make us who we are. I now know how much effort goes into writing, so I thank you for your indelible contribution to us all.

Lastly, to my fellow network marketers who treat this profession properly, and operate with integrity and ethics — I applaud you. Your success story is needed to inspire the millions of people who need to believe that joining our profession can change their lives.

TABLE OF CONTENTS

3   Become A Builder

4   Harness The Power Of The Model

5   Motivate Your Empire

6   The Mental Game

7 Modeling Your Empire

8 The Builder's Actions and Behaviors

Appendix

PREFACE

I have read many books on personal development that have helped mold me into a successful, motivated person. Much of my knowledge in network marketing came from experience out in the field, and from personal mentorship. I have found few good books on the subject — and none that were a total comprehensive blueprint that cover every important topic we must learn to become master networkers. That is why I began writing this book well over a year ago. The writing happened while I continued to be personally engaged in doing every activity you will read here. This way the information and perspective is cutting edge, not something I was reflecting on that was done a decade ago.

An important suggestion I will make to you is that you do not need to be the person who reads the most books ... but rather be the one who reads the *best* books the most. Some of my favorite books that shaped me, like *Think and Grow Rich*, I read several times. I studied them. I used them like a training manual. I would read, implement, then go back and read again. That is how this book is intended. Some of the topics here may not resonate with you at this moment, because your personal or business development is not in that place right now. Many of the ideas will surface in your business as the years progress. I promise that you will read this book five years from now and it will be a totally different experience than your first reading. You will be nodding and agreeing through the entire read. Trust me.

I will be suggesting that my team read this book once a month. Spaced Repetition is the mother of learning. It is my sincere belief that those who use this book as their main training manual and stick with the core philosophies contained within will out-earn their peers. Here's to your Building an Empire!

1

Introduction

WELCOME TO YOUR FUTURE!

The world as you have known it is about to change — not for everyone — but for those who harness the power of the network marketing business model as a catalyst of change.

The beauty of this business you've engaged in is that you are not having to pioneer something new or something that's never been done before. Actually, you should be excited that the network marketing profession has already created thousands of millionaires and countless stories of people replacing incomes, quitting their jobs to work for themselves, or creating additional income streams. Network marketing is the ultimate business model for creating *leverage* — both of time and of income. Network marketing will allow you to own a business that *you can design to fit around your life*, while a traditional business requires you to fit your life around it … and hence it *owns you*.

You are *not* entering into an abyss of the unknown. It is not that freedom has never been achieved in this business model before. There are thousands who are living the dream life already. In fact, this book will provide you the blueprint or roadmap to guide you step by step through the process to

15

achieve what the other success stories have achieved.

Can you imagine a life of complete and utter freedom? You work for no one, you are the owner of your own business, you earn income from the efforts of an army of others, you call your own shots, you have no ceiling on what you can earn, and you make a living while making a difference! Show me another way in which I can have fun, make money, and help others — all at the same time — and I am right behind you. I have never found a better way than network marketing. This business is your key to freedom.

The three ingredients required to succeed in this pursuit are:

1. Having a burning desire. You must be driven by a white-hot burning desire to accomplish your goals and succeed.

2. **Being coachable**. You must be willing to truly listen to the masters and follow their guidance with focus.

3. **Being willing to work**. You must be willing to do the work, even when you don't feel like it.

Every successful network marketer possesses *all* three. If you are missing one, you are done. It is my sincere hope and expectation that you will identity these three ingredients within you on a very conscious level.

Success is not found in convenience. Nothing worthwhile is ever easy. You will need to pay a price. You will either pay the price of hard work that begets success ... or you will refuse to make the sacrifice and pay the price of failure. Either way, a price will be paid. It is best to pay the price up front temporarily, for a lifetime of happiness. Very few people have much spare time these days. So as much as I understand the excuse we could all use that we "don't have time" to launch our business immediately, we cannot let our reasons *to do* this business become our excuse *not to*. If you *ever* want to have time freedom, then you simply cannot afford to procrastinate. If not now ... when? If not this ... what? This has to be your time. I already know this is your "what."

You have a *proven* business model. Now let's tap into the greatness that is planted inside of you and create something magnificent that you can be proud of. My goal with this book is to give to you $1 million worth of knowledge for the cost of a dinner at a medium rate restaurant. I have read several books on network marketing over my 18 years so far in this profession, but few I would recommend to my team to read. Most of the authors I read had never personally built anything substantial, at least not as big of a business that I was seeking to build. So I decided to fill that void, and give those who seek it the inside look at how I learned to build one of the industry's biggest teams. But before we begin, let me humbly say that I learned so much by gathering knowledge from so many. I was fortunate to have incredible mentors, both near and from afar. This book is my chance to pay it forward.

Since it didn't exist — and I always wished I had one — I wanted to write the ultimate, complete A-Z blueprint on *everything* it takes to go from *scratch* to a *seven-figure income* in network marketing.

This book is designed to be your "everything resource" for your entire career in building your business into an empire. My goal is for this book to be held up in the air during many top award acceptance speeches, attributing it to the massive success the industry's new top earners have experienced in their rise to the top.

THE STORY OF MONEY AND LEVERAGED INCOME

Let me start off with an important story about money, and how to control it so that it doesn't control you. I was a young man who figured out how to make seven figures a year while having complete freedom to control my own time.

- Why do you want more money?

- Why do you need more money?

- What is your relationship with money?

- Do you attract or repel money?

- What's the best way to get more money?

I grew up around money. I grew to respect money, and what it could provide for in our lives. I was raised in beautiful homes, went to incredible private schools, and was given a great university education. My parents took the family on trips around the world. I also witnessed their giving nature in helping others. I grew up learning about money from parents who understood how to play the money game. So I guess I somehow learned how to attract money, while most people seem to repel it.

I have spent much time with people who did not have

the same insight that I garnered from my upbringing. I always dreamed of someday helping many more people to be able to provide for their families what was provided for me, and what I now provide for my own family. This is why I start off with this short story about money.

What if you could get money, as an issue, out of the way in your life? No more worrying about how you will pay your bills. No more fretting over how to pay for your kids' education. No more stress over how you will afford retirement. No more staying home on vacations, driving old cars, or living in a house you don't enjoy. No more having to squelch your burning desire to give more to church and charity. Money can solve many problems in life. But you will only get more of it, *if* you learn to attract it.

Are you attracting money, or repelling it? This is important to understand. If you were conditioned and programmed your whole life that "money is the root of all evil" or "money makes people do bad things," no wonder you do not have an abundance of it. You are repelling it away from you. Subconsciously, because you do not *like* money, your actions are causing you to get rid of what money you do earn. If you can change your mind, you can change your bank account. Money is not evil, it is paper. The greed of, or doing bad things *for* or *with* the money, is the issue. Money can make you more of what you already are. If you are a bad person, you can now afford to be a worse person. If you are a good person, you can now do more nice things for others.

So decide today to respect and appreciate why money is an instrument for good. Begin to attract money rather than repel it. This mental shift will have an enormous effect on your life from today forward if you make this shift in thinking.

Decide today that you want more money, and determine what you need the money for. Then attach those *good reasons* for the need to your dominating thoughts about money. When you connect money with those reasons that compel you to *want* to earn more, you will begin to attract more.

For example, if you are a parent, you know that you have a family and children who are counting on you to be a provider. It is not acceptable to be a financial dud when others are relying on you. Not only does your financial well-being impact their lives in the *now*, but your example will set up your next generations for prosperity or failure. Right now you are sowing seeds into your children's psyche. Do not underestimate your importance. If you appreciate and teach capitalism and abundance to your family, they will grow up to continue your philosophy into the future. What will your legacy be? Will you pass on a mindset of servicing debt, or one of building wealth? As a parent do you want to spend your time being present with your children, or instead being a slave to the dollar working long hours to make ends meet? With this in mind, accept that it is imperative that you align your actions with the goal of creating wealth and gaining time freedom.

If your goal is just to earn money each month to pay bills or pay off debt, your wealth will never grow. People with this game plan often pay their bills then blow the surplus on wasteful things. But those whose goals are to earn more than their bills so that they can keep stockpiling their surplus, they are the ones who eventually live a wealthy lifestyle and bless others. Remember, you get more of whatever you focus on. Thoughts are things … so steer your thoughts. Focus on debt and you will get more of it. Focus on wealth, and you will get more of that.

How will you generate more income? In order to double your income at your job, you would likely have to double your hours. Is that possible to do? Would you even want to work that much more? Rather, what you will need to do is create a way to generate *leveraged* income — money that you earn from the efforts of others. When money comes in passively, this avails time freedom to you. But when 100 percent of your income comes from 100 percent of your efforts alone, that is a recipe for disaster. What happens if you get sick, can't work, lose your job, or want to retire? Your income is gone. Or even if you continue to work — if you keep doing what you are doing, you will keep getting what you are getting. Doing the same thing over and over expecting things to change is called insanity! So it is mandatory to employ a business model that will allow you to earn when you are not working, rather than just being an *employee* trading your time for money on a linear basis.

WHY I CHOSE NETWORK MARKETING AS MY VEHICLE TO ACHIEVE WEALTH AND TIME FREEDOM

I was programmed my entire life that multi level marketing was illegal, and people called them "pyramid schemes." So when I was introduced to them over the years, I shut them down and actually lambasted them for bothering me with such nonsense.

What is a "pyramid?"

I grew up in real estate my entire life. My father built one of the largest real estate brokerage companies on the East Coast in the 1970s, before selling it to Merrill Lynch. When my brother and I graduated from college, we both joined him in building a new real estate company. I went into sales and into opening a few offices, while my older brother went into management of the company. In sales, I was able to create a six-figure income. I worked 60+ hours a week in such pursuit. My brother worked hard too, but not in the same fashion. He focused on opening offices and recruiting others to become agents to sell houses for him. My brother never listed and sold a single house in his career, yet he out-earned me 10-to-1. He made millions because he earned a cut of every commission from all the houses his 1,000+ agents sold. He worked smarter, while I worked harder. I guess he was at the top of the "pyramid." Is this legal? Should he be allowed to earn more than any of the agents who worked so hard selling homes? I imagine everyone will agree that being a real estate broker is totally legal. Those who are smart, willing to take the financial risk of overhead, and up for the challenge of recruiting good agents, are the ones who get to live a life benefitting from leveraged Income.

So how is Network Marketing any different? I submit to you that I found it to be a step better. One day, a friend shared with me how he was earning the same income I was, but that he was doing so from home without the overhead, employees, insurance, stress, and being subject to market conditions. He was doing so in a network marketing business. At first I refuted him by denouncements that he was in a pyramid scheme. He asked me to explain why. I shared that he was earning money off the backs of others he recruited into his downline, not from his own efforts. He replied, "Do you mean like your family earns money off the backs of the real estate agents in your company?"

I froze, and anyone who knows me knows how quick-witted I normally am. Then he said, "Who is working smarter, you or your dad and brother?" Now I was mad. Not at him, but at myself. That was my light bulb moment. I had been closed-minded and it was costing me. That was the birth of my enlightenment, and I began to enter and study this network marketing profession. Let me explain why I found it to be a step better.

My research led me to learn why this business model made so much sense for a company that wanted a cost-effective way to bring a product to market. Instead of spending millions in traditional media ad buys, which has a declining effectiveness, companies are opting to employ the network marketing model. In doing so, the company only incurs marketing cost if and when a sale is made. They get an army of word-of-mouth salespeople using the most effective way of influencing buying decisions, who only get paid for performance. No salaries, only commissions. But what is also employed is a high sense of motivation, wherein these salespeople can be building a business of their own and not just be salespeople. If they choose to recruit others and teach them how to sell the product or service, they can earn override income just like the broker in a real estate company does. So now they see life through a different lens, as a business owner waking up each day excited about the future they are building for themselves. They are not salespeople; they are business owners.

Let's relate this back to my family real estate background. Our family built and owned a very large national real estate franchise. They did not work *for* the national franchisor. On the contrary, they built their own company within the umbrella of the great national, household name and support structure. In a network marketing business, you are doing the same thing — building your own business within the umbrella of the company you partner with. The marketing team you build is yours. The customer base you build with your team is yours. You have rights to the cash flow generated from your business into perpetuity.

In real estate, the agents will not likely be able to out-earn the big broker they work for. Their income is limited to only what they can personally generate. The broker is able, through massive leverage in hiring many agents, to earn substantial override commissions. How can one agent compete with that? But nowadays, many real estate companies have caught onto the merits of multilevel marketing (MLM). Instead of only one broker at the top earning off all the homes being sold by the agents they recruited, now some companies have implemented an MLM structure. Brokers have elicited the help of their agents to recruit more agents to grow their company. Agents can recruit other agents and override their sales, *without* being the broker at the top and footing the massive overhead bill. In essence, they can create their own downline network of agents within the existing structure. Some of the fastest growing brokerages have employed this model and it is the reason for their significant growth. Why? The agents would rather not just earn only from their own sales. They want *leveraged income*.

So to circle back to my story, I decided to start a networking marketing business on the side from my 60- hours-a-week real estate career. I only had a few hours a week I could devote, but I did just that. At first, I did not earn great sums of money. But I did learn a great deal. The entrepreneurial education I gained from the experience was far bigger than the initial earning I generated. But in time, my earnings grew as I grew within the profession. Now my *monthly* income from network marketing is more than I used to make *annually* in real estate. Top that off with the fact that my income is now 97 percent passive overrides and residual income from the customer base that has been built! Passive, residual income grants me the freedom to be a stay-at-home dad, to travel, and to feel in control. Now that I have lived in both worlds — traditional business and network marketing — I will never go back. Network marketing is the only way I can see for average people like me to get ahead and get control of our lives.

WHY SHOULD YOU DECIDE TO BUILD A NETWORK MARKETING BUSINESS?

In today's times, people are beginning to realize that jobs are not going to give us the lifestyle many of us desire. They are not designed to. At a job, you trade your time for money. The company will pay you just enough to get the maximum value out of you for the paycheck, and often the employee will work just hard enough not to lose the job and guaranteed income. In fact, some still believe in job security or income guarantee. As soon as your company finds someone who can do your job faster or cheaper, loyalty is out the window and you are replaced. This is hardly a way to live your life, in a constant state of worry.

Americans are finally coming to grips with the fact that they must take control of their own financial future. No President is going to fix your personal economy; only you can. The mental turning point will happen for many people once they recognize that their situation will not improve itself, and that there is a better way. Network marketing businesses allow a busy person who already has a career to start a part-time business to supplement their finances, while learning to grow the business to a larger significance. As the late business philosopher Jim Rohn taught around the world, people should work during the day earning a living, while working part time at night building their fortune. Earning a living is good, but building your own fortune is even better. Your own fortune is what will provide you with time freedom. Having control of your time allows you to live life by your own design.

The reason network marketing works is quite simple. The company wins by getting its product to the market. The consumer wins because they get access to great products or services. The network marketer wins because the company pays significant income to the middleman. But the key is the networker has pride of business ownership. The hiring, training, motivating, and selling are driven in the field by the many network marketing business builders building their own fortunes. Instead of the earning power being coddled by the select few CEOs and company owners, it is distributed out to those who are truly bringing the value to the marketplace. The more value you deliver, the more money you earn. Bring no value, earn no money. Network marketing is the finest example of capitalism.

What's great is you can find a business to start based on finding a network marketing company offering a product that you use, like, and believe in. Selling something just to sell it and earn commissions will not work well. People don't like salespeople for this reason. When you believe in what you are sharing with others, it will not seem like selling to you or them. And then you can leverage yourself into freedom by inviting others to build their own fortunes part time with you. The more people you bring aboard and teach to supplement their incomes, the higher your earnings will grow. You can now reap the rewards of the real estate broker without all of the risk and downside!

Will everyone choose to start his or her own business from home in network marketing? Of course not. There are many skeptical people who are stuck, closed-minded and would rather continue living stressed out, check-to-check, rather than venturing into something new. The very idea of making the mindset shift to becoming an entrepreneur is scary to them. They fear failing, so they will not even try. Or they may fear what others will think about them for engaging in a business that they deem as a "scheme".

You can waste your time trying to argue that the real pyramid scheme is the corporate pyramid they are currently in, where they will never earn as much as their boss or CEO. Or you can let people continue on as they wish, and stay focused on making the shift yourself and attracting wealth into your life. In time, as more and more people they respect decide to employ this network marketing business model, they may eventually come around. But it is not your job to worry about their family's finances. If they are not worried about it, then you shouldn't concern yourself with trying to help them. Everyone has freedom of choice. Don't listen to those who don't have what you want. When you buy someone's opinion, you buy their lifestyle. Rather, determine what you want and then find a mentor who has it and is willing to help you achieve what they have. You will find this mentor in network marketing like I did, because the business model compensates them for helping you win! Brilliant concept!

Just remember all of the good things you will do for people with this newfound money. Leveraged Income = Lifestyle Freedom.

MY STORY

So let me further review how my network marketing career began and blossomed into something massive. In hearing my story a little more fully, hopefully you will see that having a *big why* for succeeding was the catalyst for big success and earning more than $10 Million while in my 30s.

I grew up in a family that was built around traditional values. My parents worked very hard, and, as I mentioned earlier, built a very large real estate company in the Maryland/DC area. Growing up, I saw how hard work paid off. My father was extremely successful, and my mother was able to spend time helping him while raising us kids. We always lived in a beautiful home, had new cars, went on nice vacations, and the kids all went to private schools. I admired both my dad and mom. They worked hard, provided so much for our family, and were great examples of ambition. Sounds like the perfect picture that everyone would dream about, right? Well, what I have found is that there is always a price that is paid for success. Yes, we had it all. But that "all" included rushing to the hospital on several occasions when my father had his heart attacks caused by the stress that comes from his ambitious work life.

I was expected to take school seriously, and not getting good grades was unacceptable. My mother was always on my case, making sure I did homework immediately upon getting home from school. She was a stickler and kind of a perfectionist. I learned from her to strive for my best, and that the best was possible. I picked up the entrepreneurial spirit from my dad. Watching him build a huge real estate company, start a few banks, and owning lots of real estate investments gave me the belief that I could accomplish anything I desired. Becoming successful was not an option, as I always just knew that's what I was going to be. I could be like my dad.

Right out of college from Villanova University in Pennsylvania, I joined our family real estate company in Maryland in 1992. I worked hard from the start and made Rookie of the Year in my home county. I loved the idea of building up my business and developing my customer base. By the time I was 25 years old, I made it to the $100,000 mark. That was exhilarating! It was the result of around-the-clock effort and a determined ambition. But was I paying a high price for a high income? In a few years I would discover that I was. My older brother beat my dad's mark of having his first heart attack at 32 by doing so at 31 years of age. At the time, I was 30 and, thankfully, I was already well on my way down a different path that may have spared me from sacrificing my health for my success. After all, what good is the fortune without health?

In 1994 a friend from Villanova introduced me to network marketing. He called to tell me that someone from our class was working in a company that pays residual income and wanted to share a business opportunity with me. I told him I was too busy and not interested. He persisted and called me a few more times until I agreed to meet with them. He drove up in a new Mercedes, and I was surely impressed at age 24. That was when I discovered the power of combining leverage with residual income. I joined that company and spent 3½ years in learning mode. I say this because I certainly did not earn much money. But I fell in love with the business model, and I saw a system that made sense. There was much to learn about how to build this kind of business the right, effective way.

My path took me to another company for about a year, where I really ramped up my learning and got entrenched into personal development. It was when my second company was bought out that I discovered the right ingredients to finally hit my home run. I was ready, and I ran hard. In my first month I made $11K. My sixth month, I made $24K. My twelfth month, I made $42K, for a total of $248,000 my first year. I surpassed $500K a year within three years, and a few years later eclipsed the seven figure mark and have continued to watch it grow from there. My team had grown to more than 300,000 distributors in the first 10 years. Most importantly though, I have watched and assisted more than 1,000 people retire from their jobs due to this company, and my team (as of this writing) has been paid in excess of $300 million in commissions.

My network marketing business has enabled me to experience success in many forms. Upon earning my first million in 2½ years, I bought my million-dollar dream home in Maryland at the age of 30. The home had a gym, movie theater, spa, billiard room and huge deck for entertaining. Later that year I bought my red Ferrari 355 Spider convertible dream car. A few years later I bought property on the most beautiful tip of North Caicos Island in Turks and Caicos in the Caribbean. Then there was the Lincoln Navigator, the

Porsche, and even a brand new Bentley GT Convertible. (I still cannot believe there is a $240,000 car in my garage!) I am able to spend time as a stay at home dad for my amazing son. I go on his field trips, take him to Disney and to the islands. I now give to charities each year in excess of what I used to make in real estate. But the thing that inspires me the most is seeing the life changes happening for so many wonderful people on the team who are working together towards their goals and *achieving them*!

So it allows me to look back at the many naysayers who chastised me and scoffed that I was "getting into one of *those* things" and with pride knowing that my judgment was spot on. The best revenge is massive success. I do not fault anyone for how they have been conditioned and programmed their entire lives. Most people who speak poorly about the network marketing profession simply do not understand the business. They cannot get beyond the notions that were sewn into them by previous generations, or by the stories of pyramid schemes that someone three people removed from them lost their investment in (most likely they joined and put little effort into it, then quit). Sure, over the years some unscrupulous evildoers have created ways to scam people using schemes that look like network marketing and have soured the taste buds of many towards the business model. But that is not the norm, and it is unfortunate that it causes some people to throw the proverbial baby out with the bath water.

There is good reason why billionaires such as Warren Buffett and Donald Trump own network marketing companies. The model makes perfect sense. Pay people commissions for selling a product or a service directly to the consumer. Nobody has an issue with that. When a real estate broker gets an override commission, or a piece of the commission when one of his/her real estate agents sells a house, nobody has issue with that either. So when you combine these two models, what do you get? An ingenious way to motivate a sales force to grow itself and move product faster and more efficiently to the end consumers. Instead of the company spending all the money advertising, hiring, and training more salespeople, they let the existing reps find new salespeople to hire and train for them. Brilliant! It is by far the most cost-efficient pipeline in business today. The reason is that the word-of-mouth endorsement from someone you know influences people five times more profoundly than seeing an advertisement online or on television.

When a company sets their model up *correctly*, it is a triple win-win-win. The company's cost of sales is low, which increases profitability. The customer wins by getting a great product at a lower price than from stores that have more marketing costs and benefits provided to hire and retain employees. And the marketer (network marketer) wins by creating an income from recommending the product/service and teaching others how to effectively do so as well. The trend has grown year over year in companies electing to adopt this marketing strategy, including some of the biggest billion-dollar conglomerates in the world.

So why did I choose the network marketing model as a career path for me? Why did I decide to walk away from a very promising real estate career with our family business to build my network marketing business from home? I want to explain because I think it will resonate with you.

I knew many people who have time and *no money*, and they are unhappy. I knew many who have money and *no time*, and they are unhappy. I knew few who have both time and money together, which creates true *freedom*. That was what I was after. In real estate, I felt like I would never be able to let up off the gas pedal to enjoy life without my income slowing down too. In the real estate business as a broker, I would be the only one getting to benefit from leverage when the agents made sales. I felt bad that the agents were all on perpetual treadmills, with the one broker getting the chance to earn from other people's efforts. So if I recruited an agent to come work for us selling houses, I was simply helping them onto the treadmill. That didn't sit well with me, especially now that I knew of a better way.

I was also attracted to the promise of *residual* income in network marketing. In real estate we are only as good as our next sale. We wake up every single morning unemployed until our next sale. Once a house is sold, it's back to "first and ten" all over again. When would this ever end? There is no residual. In network marketing, I loved the idea that I could sign up a customer *one time*, yet get paid a commission on that sale month after month *for the life* of the customer. I met people in my current company who had signed up customers one time back in the 1970s and '80s. They are still getting paid residuals today — *decades* later! Who would not get excited about that?

WHY RESIDUAL INCOME IS SO IMPORTANT

I have said for years that most people just don't understand what *residual* income really is. This term gets tossed around quite a bit. But few actually have it. I would rather have $100,000 a year of residual income coming in year after year, passively, than $250,000 a year that I have to slave away for every day. The money you have to keep chasing will stop when you stop … and eventually you will stop. Residual income is money that you keep receiving on a continual basis after doing something one time. I call it "Elvis Presley money" because Elvis' estate is still receiving residuals today on songs he recorded and movies he appeared in from 40 years ago! He is still one of the top income earners in the country … decades after he passed. *That* is residual income.

There are a few ways to create residual income for yourself:

- Be a music recording artist

- Write best-selling novels

- Be a famous actor

- Sell insurance

- Buy and rent real estate

- Build a network marketing business that has a recurring/subscription model.

For the first three, the odds are stacked against you and me. I can't sing, I don't want to write fiction, and acting is not going to work out for me. I could sell insurance, but man, so much competition — not to mention a very grueling career grinding out sales.

Let's compare the last two options. Assume your desire is to create $2,000 a month in residual cash flow. Here is what it will take using these options:

Real Estate Investment — If you buy a home with a mortgage of $250,000 and your monthly payment is, say, $1,500. Let's assume you can rent this home out for $2,000 a month. This gives you a $500/month gross residual income (before taking out any expenses like repairs, commissions, advertising, etc., which adds up). So you would need to take out $1,000,000 in loans to buy 4 houses to generate $2,000/month gross.

Network Marketing — Join a company you believe has a great product/service for less than $500 one-time fee. Recruit five others and teach them to duplicate just two times (5 + 25 + 125). You now have a team of 155 people marketing that product/service that you are getting paid on. In just about any network marketing company comp plan that is designed properly, you should be generating $2,000/month in income from the sales made by your team. So not only is this income passive (sales made by others and not you) but if the company has a model where you sign up a customer one time and they keep making payments every month without having to repeatedly make another sale to them — you have *true* residual income. So we are talking about an investment of less than $500 and some part-time sweat equity and there is no limit to how big your residuals can grow.

Few have the ability to invest a fortune in real estate to create this, but anyone can do it using the network marketing business model using leverage.

Let me explain the concept of leverage using the following diagram:

RS

JRS

)URS

(YOU ARE GETTING PAID FOR
AS THE RESULT OF LEVERAGE)

Are you are willing to carve out five hours a week to build your network marketing business?

Now let's help you recruit five people who are also willing to do the same … (5 x 5 hrs. = 25 hours).

And we will help those five each recruit five more (25 x 5 hrs. = 125 hours).

So you now have you, plus 30 others, each working five hours per week. So *you* are getting paid on 155 man hours per week, yet you are still only putting in five hours a week yourself. This is called leverage — getting paid on the efforts of more than just your own. Billionaire J. Paul Getty once said, "I'd rather get paid 1 percent off the efforts of 100 people, than getting paid 100 percent of just my own effort."

WILL IT BE WORTH IT?

To you, my readers who have likely started down your path of building a business in network marketing, I must address the inevitable. You will often question whether the "juice will be worth the squeeze." I wish I had counted the times over the last 17 years that I felt like quitting. When I first got into this industry, it looked so simple, easy, and exciting. I had no idea that I was going to go through an amazing amount of personal growth and development. I wasn't expecting so many people to tell me no, and so many of those who joined me would soon quit. The challenge lies in the setting of expectations. If we are prepared ahead of time for such challenges, we will be ready for them when they come. And we will know exactly *why* they will come, and therefore lessen their impact on us.

A great analogy for this is when Mormon churches send out young men on missionary work to knock on doors to spread their message. If the kids were just told to go out and spread the word without warning them what they will likely encounter and why, the first time a door is slammed in their face (or mean-spirited language was spoken to them) they would likely give up and quit. Since the church knows that these kids need to be prepared for such an onslaught of belittling obstacles, they do something very brilliant. They bring the youth in to inoculate them before sending them out — letting them know to expect the slammed doors and the hateful things they will be told. More importantly they are told *why* these people will do such things. Now that the young men *expect* such rejection, when they encounter it — it does not deflate them. They expect it and grasp it! It allows them to push through and keep going forward.

Are your *reasons* for succeeding in your business bigger than the pain of enduring rejection and the growing pains? *WHY* are you doing this business in the first place? I like to say "If your *WHY* is strong enough, you will stick around long enough and endure all that you must to learn how to succeed."

So what is your *why*? Your *why* isn't just about money, but rather what will the money do in your life once you get it? If you had $10 million right now, what would be the most immediate things you would do? Some say they would quit their job and spend more time with their family. Some would start a charity. Some would retire their parents or build them a new home. Some would build their dream home or travel the world. Some would finally follow their passion and write music or pen a book.

Write down YOUR WHY here:

_____

_____

_____

_____

_____

_____

_____

_____

_____

If you say you are doing this for your kids, which is stronger — your desire to avoid some no's, or your love for your kids? How many people telling you *no* will cause you to quit and not give your kids their parents back?

If you want to retire your parents, how many *no's* will make you say, "I've had enough, my parents can just keep on working?"

You see, when your Why is incredibly strong, it will give you the will to withstand much more than you can possibly imagine. Most people who quit on their network marketing business do so because they never truly connected with their purpose — their *WHY* — in the first place.

QUITTERS NEVER WIN.
WINNERS NEVER QUIT ... THEY FINISH WHAT THEY START.
"I WILL ... UNTIL!"

I wrote this on my wall in my home office.

YOUR NETWORK MARKETING BUSINESS VS. YOUR JOB

When speaking at major events across the country through the years, I often ask the audience, "Whatever you do right now for a living, if you were the Michael Jordan of your profession —if you were the very best at doing that job, and you do it better than anyone else out there for the next 20 years — how many of you will you be able to retire at the end of those 20 years with your *dream lifestyle*?" I look around and rarely does a single hand go up. I follow up with, "So what you are telling me is that there is no chance that your job will ever provide you with the lifestyle you dream about? Even if you were the very best at it, you still won't achieve your dreams in 20 years? Yet you still give that job 8-10 hours every day, going down that road, knowing there is no light at the end of the tunnel?" And the looks on their faces are always of enlightenment mixed with dismay.

Then I ask, "On the other hand, if you hit the top level in our network marketing business, and you are making a quarter million dollars a year or more, passively, and you have time freedom to call your own shots and live life on your own terms … how many of you feel that you could live the life you dream about?" And without fail *every* hand goes up. I iterate, "So your *job* does not even offer the chance to live your dreams … but this business does! *Remember this always*! So why would you ever think your job is more important in your life than your own network marketing business? Now I'm not recommending that you run and quit your job tomorrow. Of course not. Keep your job and earn your living during those hours, while in your off-hours you build your fortune. Down the road, you may find that your part-time business income eclipses what you make at your job. At that point you have options!"

Awareness is key. I hold that many people are programmed by society to believe that having a job is noble, and that working a hard day for someone else is responsible. Most people I know do not feel like the work they do at their job is in alignment with their purpose or their passion in life. They feel unhappy, stressed out, underpaid, under-appreciated, tired, and fatigued. The reason is because as humans we all seek *congruence*. When the things we are passionate about and want out of life are not connected to the work that we do, we have a sense of brokenness. We are not congruent. So now that you know what your *why* is, and you know that your job cannot provide it, but your network marketing business can, how will this change your life?

Bethany Hamilton, the 13-year-old whose story of losing her arm in a shark attack while surfing was the basis for the hit movie "Soul Surfer," had the kind of mindset that all networkers need to adopt. After the attack, she told her father she wanted to compete in surfing again without her arm. Her father said "It won't be easy," and her response was, "I don't want easy, just *possible*." The good news: ultimate success and your dream lifestyle *are possible* with your network marketing business!

Success in this business will take sacrifice. Freedom is not free. Everyone who is very successful and living at the mountaintop has paid a hefty price to get there. Since most people are still working a full-time job and building their business part-time in the evenings and weekends, those hours are now your most valuable commodity. Prior to starting your business, those were your slacking hours to play and have fun. But now you have a different outlook. You will have to borrow from your bowling night, or your movie night, or your football games to invest that time into what is going to make your life better. If you only have four hours a week to devote, then you must devise a strategy to make those four hours count. They must be the most productive, passion-charged hours of your entire week!

Belief is a critical factor in our ability to remain excited and passionate about our business. This belief is what is going to attract others whom we are trying to recruit. *Belief* in the Company, the Product, the Upline, the Opportunity and Yourself.

> • If you do not have 100 percent belief in the company and product you chose, then it is time for an immediate assessment. Of course, no company or product will be perfect, but you still must believe that the company is strong, financially sound, and has your best interest at heart. The product/service must be something that you would buy even if you were not in the business of selling it.

• You must be convinced that there are plenty of examples of distributors succeeding in the business to warrant your belief that "If they can do it, I can do it, too." The compensation plan needs to be balanced in that it pays well for those just getting started, as well as the rewards for those who reach the top being worth the effort.

• Does your upline know what they are doing and are they effective at teaching others to accomplish their goals? We all need to believe in the person(s) we are following. Do they have integrity, work ethic, and are they worthy of modeling? Are they accessible to you? Search upline until you find the right person to follow.

• This leads us to self-belief. Do you believe that you deserve success? Do you feel you are willing to learn what you do not know? Do you expect that, with the right coaching, you can make it to the top of your company? Confidence is key — and it cannot exist without being born from belief in all five components. The company, product, upline, and comp plan are all fixed constants in your business that you cannot change. The difference between those who succeed in your company and those who don't is the "You Factor." That is what this book is about ... we are going to Empower *you* to be the ultimate network marketer. You are going to take the same four constants and set some new records in your company! We have to work on you.

THE LEARNING CURVE

When you first start your business, your knowledge is low and your anxiety is likely high. This is not a very good mix, but it is expected. This is not a get-rich-quick scheme or a lottery. This is a business, and it will take some time to learn it. This learning curve's time frame will be different for everyone. You can shorten the curve by compressing the learning activity faster. Attending more training classes offered by top earners in your company, reading books (like this one), listening to conference calls and CDs — all of this will help. Just remember that an hour in the field is worth 20 hours in the classroom. We all have to be in classroom mode some of the time, but unless we go into the real world to try and apply it, nothing will happen.

After coaching countless people at this point, one thing is clear. People love to try to build this business their own way. They come to the business with skill sets and strategies that pertain to completely different industries, and they try to apply them to this business model. This is often met with frustration as they realize their ideas don't work so well here. I *was one* of *these people too*! Network Marketing is a different animal than what they were used to. In corporate America, management has always driven business forward. In the new era, and in this profession, leadership is far more important. This business is all about using tools, using a system, leveraging the help and credibility of your third party upline expert, and taking everything completely off of you. Again, this is the opposite of what many expect. Salespeople think they should come in and just go do it all by themselves. This may work a little bit, but it sure doesn't duplicate. And this business is *all* about *duplication*.

There are certain how to's we need to learn in this

business:

- Listening skills

- Presenting the product/service

- Approaching prospects to pique interest to recruit

- Relating to objections

- Motivating our team

- Servant leadership

- Training our recruits to follow the system

- Creating urgency and fear of loss with prospects to move them to join

- Time management

- Contact management and follow up skills

- Problem solving

Over time, these things can be learned. The more you are in activity mode out there talking to prospects and recruiting/selling, the more your skills will be honed. Ninety percent of our business will not be learned by reading a training manual. Certainly the reading must happen, but it will not make much sense until you are out there in the marketplace experiencing it firsthand. I call it "failing forward". I eventually loved messing up, because I learned from it. Every time

I did not connect with a prospect properly, I examined the conversation and asked "what could I have said or not said that might have better attracted his attention?" Or when a new recruit did not follow the system or quit right away, I asked myself, "What might I have done differently to get him to take one more step in the business and help him on the path towards a win?"

I was told by my mentor to expect a five-year growth curve. After five years of consistently building and learning, I will have a foundation of knowledge (from the classroom) and wisdom (from real experience) on which I can build a life-lasting business in this industry. It is amazing how true that turned out to be.

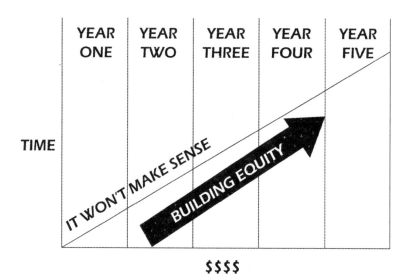

INVEST TIME TO GET A BIG RETURN

Was it worth five years of focused effort to learn this

business? You have read my story, I will let you decide. Yes, we "earn while we learn" in network marketing. So I did earn good income fairly early on. But the rewards come in the form of a compounded effect. You earn smaller amounts in the beginning while you are working for hours in learning mode so that down the road in five years you are earning large amounts without many hours being required to sustain that income. This truly should be seen as a five-year game plan.

One more *important* aspect of learning in this business of yours; the more you learn and know about your business, the more you will tend to *talk* (and not rely on third-party tools and people). And when this happens, expect your results to go *down*! This warning must be understood and heeded. Yes, you want to learn all that you can. But having the knowledge, and spewing it out there at every chance you get, are two completely different things. Knowledge will certainly be very beneficial, as it breeds confidence inside of you. But there are times to use it, and times to just let your posture feed off of it.

You will learn in this book that when it comes to recruiting your own prospects, less is more. Say *less* to *more* people, and take the focus off of you. You do not want your prospects to think they need all the knowledge that you possess in order to join and be successful. But you *will* definitely get to use your knowledge outwardly when you are the third-party expert for your team down the road.

SELF DOUBT

Warning: There will be many, many times when you will doubt whether the business works, or whether there is something wrong with you for not succeeding faster. Let's nail this down right now. The business *does work* … just look at all the people in your company who are experiencing amazing success. Again, it comes down to the *you factor* discussed earlier. Knowing this, you will tend to self-assess constantly when you are not succeeding fast enough. By the way, it is subjective how you define "succeeding" or even "fast enough." You may find that you're comparing yourself to others in your company in an unhealthy way. It is OK to measure your business against someone else to see how you can improve in different areas. But do not let yourself fall into the trap of comparing yourself with others if it makes you get down on yourself. I did this for years. You do not know what head start that person may have had in the network marketing industry. You don't know if they followed the system better, how many books they read, or if they got really good at one of the skills in the business where you need attention.

The reality is that you can do this business and win. It all starts with your *belief*. If you have it, then you can have *confidence*. This is critical, because without confidence you cannot have *influence*. And influence is what moves people. I repeat: *Influence* is *what moves people*.

We are in a people-moving business. We move prospects to join. We move distributors to do activity to sell/recruit. Influence can be learned by tracing it backwards. Keep working on your belief, and that will build your confidence, and as your confidence grows — the more influential you will become.

Why do people quit on their business, on their dreams?

Everyone has a different "IQ level." In other words, what it takes for someone to say "I Quit" varies. Those who have weak *why*'s often quit before they even begin. They sign up on a Tuesday and by Wednesday they have already joined the Witness Protection Program! Who knows what they were thinking when they joined, what their motivation was, or even what values were instilled into them as children. Unfortunately, many parents do not realize the damage they do to their kids by allowing them to quit things that they start. If you "tried" soccer, baseball, karate, basketball, swimming, an instrument — and were allowed to quit because you didn't become amazing at them in the first week — no wonder why it is hard to engage and stay committed to a new business (or even a relationship or marriage).

Yes, people quit their network marketing business for various reasons. There are two rules of thumb to live by:

1. Never quit on yourself!

2. Try to keep people from quitting, learn from those who do, but never let it derail you when someone does!

The only person you can control is you. Others will do what they want, and if their *WHY* was not strong enough to keep them in the game, that's on them.

What can you do to anchor your recruits in the business?

• Introduce them via welcome calls to other success stories in the business in their first 48 hours

• Share the *vision* of the company several times in their first week

• Sell them on their *dream/why* again and again every few days

• Get them more passionate about the product/service by sharing testimonials, and urge them to be a product of the product themselves

• *Get them* a *commission check immediately* — Their "Belief Check"

• Make them feel appreciated and a part of a team (people are less likely to quit on a team than they will quit on themselves)

• Build a personal relationship with them.

Just do your best to be a servant leader. People don't care how much you know, until they know how much you care. When you put the needs and desires of your downline before yourself, it will be noticed. As Zig Ziglar says, "Help enough other people get what they want in life, you will get more than what you want."

So what about you ... the one person you *can* control? How can you keep yourself from the decision to give up when the going gets tough? To set your expectations properly, I want you to know that things will be tough at times. We all hit dry spells when we just can't seem to recruit anyone for weeks or more. Maybe your business is not growing as fast as others' are. Maybe you have friends or family members who are taking shots at you, telling you that you are a fool for even trying to build your own business to get ahead in life. Maybe they are attacking your company, or even the network marketing model. Trust me, I got this from all angles for years!

Like I said earlier, their ignorance was not going to stop me from achieving my dreams. Their pictures were not on my dream board, and they certainly were not going to pay my bills or fund my dream life. So I had to develop my *rhino skin*. Most people who quit have "baby skin," meaning they feel every little prod, jab, or disappointment. It hurts badly because their skin is so soft. A rhino (if you have seen them on TV) can have a bird land on its back and even peck with its beak, and the rhino does not even feel it. This is because to withstand the elements and to avoid being prey for other animals, it develops a very thick skin. As your belief in your business and in yourself rises, your skin will get thicker. The verbal attacks and the rejection you will face will stop hurting so much, and will someday just bounce right off. Will you enjoy the jabs and the rejection? Not really, but you will understand why it comes, you will expect it, and you will plow right through it! Believe me, it gets easier and easier.

How can you develop your rhino skin?

• Attend every company event you can
• Listen to leaders on conference calls
• Listen to as many success stories as you can
• Read personal development books (10 pages every day)
• Read books about the network marketing industry

We'll develop some of these concepts in the ensuing chapters.

2

The System

STARTING YOUR BUSINESS VS. LAUNCHING IT

So you decided to join this company. You filled out an application and invested your money. Now what?

Well, it's time to get started — or maybe time to start over from scratch. But what's the difference between *starting* and *launching*? This is simple, but powerful when understood. The difference is *slow* versus *fast*. And the important fact to note is that *this business is way easier and more effective to build fast than slow.* This is a momentum business, and the faster it's built, the easier it is to create and maintain momentum. Let's explore …

If your goal is to present your opportunity to 20 people, which of the following strategies is best?

1. Sit down and present to each of the 20 one at a time over 20 days?

2. Invite all 20 to a one-hour presentation on one day?

Of course, everyone will agree that #2 is by far the best strategy. But why?

• Saves 19 hours of your time through leverage

• Compresses time frames so you make more money faster (better story)

• Creates synergy by building in waves of people

• You are teaching leverage to those you recruit in the process

• Your business will grow exponentially instead of by addition / one at a time

So by launching your business, you spend less time, earn more, and you set in motion a ripple effect that will multiply these results and help you become a top earner in your company. *What you do duplicates.* If you start slow, so will your team. If you launch, so will your team. Half of the training of your new recruits already happened in the process of them signing up. What they saw you do with them, they will do with their prospects.

A good example of starting vs. launching would be a plane getting ready to take off on the runway. Let's say this plane is getting ready to leave Los Angeles and fly to New York. At the end of the 2,000 feet of runway is a patch of trees. The plane needs to get lift and get over those trees. So let's say the pilot goes about 25 percent throttle. Will it make it? No. How about 50 percent throttle? No. How about 70 percent? In these scenarios that plane will be smashed into those trees. Only at 100 percent throttle will that plane get off the ground and into the sky. Once it is up to a "cruising altitude," only then will the pilot throttle back to, say, 50 percent. If not, the fuel will not last and the plane will go down somewhere in Missouri. You see, a plane needs to go all out to start its journey, but it cannot continue at that pace forever. It does not need to … nor does your business.

Let's talk about momentum. Momentum is hard to get, and easy to lose. It is best understood when you think of the plane in cruise mode. Much energy/fuel was spent getting the plane into flight. But once flying, it takes far less fuel to get you to your destination. Your network marketing business will be the same way. A sudden burst of consistent energy will launch you, and then applying a constant but lesser effort will sustain your growth and your income. And at future intervals, you can surely add new bursts of energy to go to new levels.

Another analogy to convey the importance of being *consistent* in your business efforts is the *water pump*. To get water out of a deep well with an old-fashioned water pump, you start pumping the lever. You pump, and pump, and pump until the water finally starts flowing. Once the flow starts, it takes less forceful and less frequent pumps to keep it flowing. And that water will keep coming as long as your hand keeps that lever moving. That is exactly true to form in your network. At the beginning, it's your hand on the lever pumping hard and fast. Soon enough, you can ratchet back a little, but you cannot let that water retreat back down the pipe. Eventually, once you have developed some great leaders on your team, you will be able to put their hands on the lever to keep the flow going so you can have more time freedom without your income flow stopping.

The great thing about momentum is that is can make an average networker (like me!) look really good! Even if you are not a master at this business, momentum fills in your gaps. It does much of the heavy lifting for you. So the take-away is this: *Once you have some momentum, do whatever you must to keep it going*! At the first sign of momentum, double up your efforts and your communication with your team. The fatal mistake 95 percent of networkers make is thinking when their business starts rocking, that it's OK to let up off the gas pedal expecting business to just soar to the moon. In actuality, that's when your most promising work really begins and your efforts should be doubled or tripled.

BE SYSTEM DRIVEN

One thing I know *for sure*: Every networker I have watched fall short of success, it is because they did not follow The System. And I have witnessed some make it to the top, only to fall from there by ceasing to do what got them there. The *biggest* key to success in network marketing is commit-ting 100 percent to the system.

Networkers who have built massive organizations learned the distinction between *System Driven* versus *People Driven.*

When you are "people driven," it means that every-thing hinges on *your* involvement. Meetings only happen when *you* host them. Presentations only happen when *you* present. Your downline gets trained when *you* train them. That sounds like one heck of a treadmill to me! I imagine that you started this business because you ultimately want freedom, not another job. So the only way to achieve true time freedom lies in the fact that the business must be built to rely on a system and *not you.*

You must adopt a "system driven" philosophy. Everything you do must be scalable, meaning it can be copied and duplicated by the masses. This is what will allow your team to grow into the thousands, then to the hundreds of thousands. An infrastructure of meetings, presentations, and trainings should be set in place for all of your team to plug into. It is predictable, reliable, and effective. In a later section, we will also discuss why third-party is so crucial to your success. You do not want your team to rely solely on you, as the full weight of that will crush you. The key is for them to rely on The System, so in the future when you want to go on vacation or retire, your business will keep on building without you!

To understand the power in being system driven, picture a fast-moving river. Let's say your goal is to get people downriver. You can choose to put one person on your shoulder and physically carry them on foot along the riverbank. That will get tiring, and you can only handle one person at a time. Your second option would be to throw people into the river and let the current sweep them all the way down to your destination *for you*. The great news is that there is no limit to the number of people you can put into the river. The current (The System) will carry as many as you can find. But if you are not in the river yourself, and are just throwing people in, they might just try to climb out to join you on the riverbank (outside of The System). So better yet, be sure *you* are in the river (in The System) too, so that you can be swept right along with your team.

In most cases, The System has already been put in place for you by your upline top earner, or by your company. If not, it may be your time to step up and become that leader who launches it. But first, explore what is already in place through your mentors.

SYSTEM COMPONENTS

Here is what my System looks like that built my team to more than 300,000 people.

The System		
1. Get Excited 2. Make your list 3. Book a PBR (within first 3-5 days) 4. Book a PCC (within first 3-5 days) 5. Weekly Business Briefing 6. Trainings (Events and Calls) 7. Corporate Convention	**P** **L** **U** **S**	- Conference calls - Sit-downs - Three-ways calls - Long-distance packages - Webinars

Let's break this down piece by piece:

Get Excited — Most people say they are excited about starting their new network marketing business, but you would never know that by talking to them. They don't really come across as passionately fired up about it, or about life. The reason this will ensure their failure is because we are in a people-attraction business. If you are not excited, why would anyone else want to do what you are doing? So you have to work on *your music*. This is how you sound when you are communicating with people. Are people attracted to your tone, to your ambition and outlook? Or do people sense that you are stuck in a spot that they would rather not join you in being stuck themselves? It's not about "fake it 'til you make it." You don't need to fake anything … just be genuinely excited about your product/service, your opportunity, and your future success! Act and feel presently how you see yourself living in the future. This will be attractive to others. People want to follow someone who knows where they are going, and is inspiring to be around! It's *not just the how* to's *that matter* … it's *how you* do *the how* to's *that makes the difference.* Your attitude will determine your paycheck. Get a positive attitude and be enthusiastic about everything you do.

Make your List — So whom do you plan to contact and invite to review your opportunity or product/service? Without a list of people to call, you have no business. Our companies pay us amazing commissions for our endorsement to the people who trust our endorsement. That is why network marketing (direct-selling) works better than any other sales platform in the world. If you truly believe in what you are marketing, you will *want* to share it with everyone you know and care about. So write down the names of everyone you have ever met in your life (seriously!). The average list for someone over 25 years old should be in excess of 200 people. But let's start with 50, and add to it in the days to come. Next, you want to grade your list — determine which people you want to lead with the product/service, and which you want to lead with the business opportunity. This list is your goldmine. It will only give you gold if you mine it!

Book your PBR — A PBR is a Private Business Reception. This is a living room presentation at your home. PBRs are proven to be the most effective way to launch your business. Do not delay. This should be done in your first three to five days in the business. In a previous chapter, we discussed why you want to *launch* your business fast by presenting to a group of people all at once. This is how you will do it.

Your goal is to invite everyone you know in your home-town over to your home for a short 40-minute overview. Just like we have baby showers or Super Bowl parties, this will be similar. It is an informal environment where people can feel comfortable, and it's easy to invite to. To reiterate, when you have a group of prospects all seeing the presentation at once (either done live by your sponsor, or by playing a DVD), it makes for incredible synergy and excitement. Once someone catches the vision and shows signs of interest, it often turns into a domino effect and becomes contagious. Next thing you know, people are filling out their applications.

The keys to a successful PBR are:

- **Be enthusiastic.** They are buying into you as much as they are the company or product/service. At the beginning, the *host* should share *why* they looked at this business in the first place (lack of money, lack of time, etc). Do this in a way so it resonates with your audience and connects your *why* with *theirs*. Hit them emotionally.

- **Keep the presentation brief.** If you get long-winded, you will lose people.

- **Facts tell, stories sell**. Be sure to share product and opportunity testimonials.

- **Paint the vision** of the magnitude of the business you and the people in the room can build together and how it will enable each person's success to meet the needs of their own *why*. They need to feel like they will be part of something bigger than themselves, and that they will have plenty of support in the process.

- **At the end, don't invite questions.** You will get what you ask for. Ask for questions, you'll get questions. Instead, "assume the sale" by having the posture ... *of course they will sign up*! If anyone has questions, answer them privately off to the side so as not to distract others from filling out their applications. Just get people filling out applications to join! Don't be weak or timid about it (but don't be pushy either). Have a relaxed intensity.

- **Have applications and pens ready.** If using a laptop or tablet, have it ready to go.

- For those you recruit, book *their* PBR in their homes for the upcoming week *before* they leave!

Book your PCC — A PCC is a Private Conference Call. This is like a telephonic PBR or business presentation. It is a way to present your business to multiple prospects at one time, in 15 minutes, right over the phone! Don't delay on this one, either. This should also be done in your first three to five days in the business. And best yet ... you can have a top producer (expert in the company) do the presentation on the call to your prospects *for you*! Of course you want to do a living room meeting (PBR) for the people in your hometown, but for everyone else who cannot attend in person at your home, you set a date and time and invite them to listen in over a phone line.

PCCs are designed for each distributor to do separately, for *their* prospects only. We do not recommend several distributors combining onto one call. If this is done, each will usually get only a few guests on, and get small results. By doing a PCC for every newly recruited person independently, that new person will have the chance to invite all of their friends, family, and colleagues into one informal and intimate setting ... and everyone will feel comfortable and relaxed. But they will get to hear a powerhouse, personalized presentation!

Here's how you do it: The date and time of the call is decided upon, usually with about a one- or two-day notice. The upline will provide the conference call number for everyone to dial in on (you can find companies online that offer free conference call lines). Always invite three times the amount of people that you expect to actually show up on the call. Invite and confirm 30 to get 10 on. The purpose of these calls is to create excitement and to share your business opportunity with many people as quickly as possible. So the PCC should be treated with major urgency and importance.

To invite people to the call:
"Hey Bill, it's _____. Look, I don't know if you knew this, but I needed a change, so I have been investigating businesses that might excite me. I ran across a business expert who has turned me onto something pretty big. It may be the biggest thing I have ever seen from a profit standpoint, and the ability to do so while having some quality time freedom. The person I met is going to talk about this on a private conference call tomorrow night at 8 p.m. and I asked if it was OK

for you to listen in with me. You have *GOT* to hear what's going on ... so get on this call for 15 minutes! Grab a pen and write down this time and phone number. Be sure to call in a minute early. See you on there!"

To host the call: Call in three minutes early, and personally welcome your friends you've invited. Ask for their name as they call in (write them down so you know who to follow up with personally after the PCC ends). Tell them you are glad they could join in, and that the call will start at [the designated time] sharp! When that time comes, introduce the speaker.

"Everyone, I am so glad you took 15 minutes to be on this call. You will thank me after, I promise you! I want to introduce you to [expert's name] who is leading the national expansion of this powerhouse company, who knows all the facts and knows how to make massive money in this arena, and loves to help people. Mr./Ms. _____, take it away!"

The speaker will go 15 minutes, and then direct everyone back to the Host to get signed up. The Host should take the calls from those who call them, but if the phone does not ring, start making follow-up calls that same night to close them while they are hot! If they still have questions, then initiate a three-way call with the expert privately to get the answers, and get them closed.

NOTE: If you have no upline speaker to do your PCC, do everything the same way, but instead, say,

"We are so lucky, we are going to patch in and listen to a conference call with a top executive that's getting ready to start. Hold on for one second ..." Then three-way the line into a recorded overview number from your upline. After the recording is done, disconnect, then start making follow-up calls to see who is interested by asking, "What did you like best about what you heard?" If they still have questions, then three-way them into the expert privately to get the answers, and get them closed.

Congratulations. You now know the secret to exploding your business. Some people don't do PCCs, and that's why their income is not as high. The next step is duplicate ... get every new recruit on your growing team to do their PBR and PCC in their first three to five days too!

Your business is officially launched! These next steps are to be regular ongoing activities.

Attend your weekly business briefing. Most successful network marketing companies understand the importance of human interaction, and the need for people to come together. A "business briefing" is where a leader will rent a room at a local hotel and conduct a PowerPoint presentation about the opportunity for any guests that the existing team can invite to come. This is such a powerful way to recruit on an ongoing basis *after* you have launched your business with your PBR and PCC. This business is all about contacting and inviting. You need an event to invite people to, where a third-party expert with credibility can present the information to your prospects *for you*. And again, like the PBR, the synergy and excitement comes from the numbers of others in the room.

One of the common questions I am asked is why reps need to come out to a business briefing every week to see the same presentation, often the same speakers with the same jokes, over and over again. Why attend, especially if they have no guests to bring with them to see the overview? "I don't like meetings" is often heard.

Is attending every week *that* important to someone's success in the business? *Yes*! Here's why.

1. Often times, people get recruited via a one-on-one meeting, with a flip chart, website, conference call, or DVD. This is great that an individual at any place, any time, can recruit people. But you do not ever want to leave that new recruit with their view of the company being limited to just you or a simple "tool" they reviewed. That completely scales down the much larger picture and vision of the company. Your company is a people business, a movement. Can you imagine if Martin Luther King Jr. did not have a large crowd to speak to with his powerful and dynamic message, but rather sat with one person at a time with a DVD? "I Have a Dream" would never have been heard, and the echoes of those profound words would not have shaken the world.

2. This is why you need to attend the "assembly," the events where the team comes together. Your prospects and new recruits need to be there too. This paints the bigger picture, where they not only catch the vision of the company's mission, but they also realize while at the meeting that they are a part of something bigger than themselves. This is powerful, and important. People are more moved to act when they feel important, that their efforts

are for a greater cause.

3. Sometimes "life happens" and you can easily get distracted from your network marketing business. Maybe your business has a lull, or maybe your morale is down and you need a lift. So you come to the weekly meeting to get around the positive people who are having tons of success and excited about their life, and you too will re-catch the vision. Your fire will be fueled … which we *all* need on a regular basis to keep charging ahead. Rejection and disappointment is a part of business, but in *this* business we can weather those storms more easily because we can get around and feed off those who are having up days and big success. Sometimes you *need* the meeting, and other times if you are doing great, the others at the meeting need *you*! Think of *team* as an acronym for *Together Everyone Achieves More.*

4. You will be able to introduce your prospects to others they can relate to, from a similar background, for example. Quite often, that could be the catalyst that convinces someone that they, too, can do this business. There is no substitute for a powerful, live event.

5. How will you ever learn how to do a presentation yourself? The best way is by sitting in front of it about 50 times. This will re-sell you and increase your belief and confidence. It will help you get the lingo and language down. And soon

you will be able to properly share the stories in a compelling way that will help you sell and recruit like the masters who make million-dollar incomes. It really is amazing that some people claim that they are too busy, too tired, or too whatever to be at a meeting for one hour once a week. With travel time, let's call it two hours. Over the course of a year, that's barely over 100 hours! Many people work that much in two weeks at their *JOB* (an acronym for "Just Over Broke") working tirelessly building someone else's dreams and lifestyle — and never even get the chance to get the massive six-figure income and time freedom! Yet they find excuses why they can't invest a few hours each week for just a few years in order to create a huge residual income and change their life. Amazing, isn't it?

6. Finally, briefings give you a place to bring prospects to recruit new people on board on an ongoing basis.

The great thing is, if you bring your guests out, they will see the big picture and at the same time recognize they can come back for all the above reasons. They will also use this venue to grow their team and business. This is called duplication. This is The System. This is called *leverage*. Poor people *get* leveraged. Rich people *use* leverage. You and your team get to use these weekly meetings to leverage other people's testimonials, presentation skills, inspiration, and collective synergy to explode your business. And best yet, these weekly meetings are being held (or can be) in nearly every marketplace across the map! So as your team grows away from you, they will have the same support *system* available to them. And as they are building in their markets, you are still at *your* local meeting — but making money in your pocket from hundreds of meetings going on every week! The event is motivating them without you even being present!

So now you know why you and your team want to plug into business briefings, right? So how many briefings will you attend this year? If you said "52," that would be correct! And how many people do you want to recruit and plug into these events? Thousands, I hope! Start going to your local briefing, and get fanatical about it. Don't let your friends, family, or negative dream-stealers talk you out of going. They *will* try, but will you let them? The rain or cold may come, but you will go anyway. Your favorite sports team will play on the same night, but you will realize this is *your* game day, and you will be dressed and on the field playing for *your* championship ring! THIS is one of your most important *core commitments*. Get committed and get wealthy.

Attend training events. Training is the key to your success. That is why you are reading this book. You may have heard the phrase "Knowledge is Power." This is not fully accurate. I believe that *applied knowledge* is *power*. What good is knowing something, but not doing anything about it? You know how great your product/service is. You know how your opportunity can change people's lives. But that is not enough. The key is learning how to transfer your belief to others. This is just one of the concepts that require *training*.

"Practice makes perfect," right? Maybe not! What if you keep practicing doing something the wrong way? Will you succeed? Not likely. You will just get better at failing. The key is getting training on the right way to do it first, then practice, and then see what you can tighten up and improve. I call it *plan-do-review*. Your company provides training classes taught by those who are great at the business. Their goal is to empower you by showing you what works, as well as what doesn't work. This way you can cut your learning curve down drastically.

PLAN – Get trained and learn the techniques and strategies that work.

DO – Go out in the field and implement what you've learned. Do the activity.

REVIEW – Come back to the classroom to sharpen your axe and see if there are areas you can improve.

This is a cycle. We are never done learning. Either we are growing, or we are dying ... getting ripe or getting rotten. I made a vow to myself to never stop learning and getting better. What I have found is that *most people fail in their network marketing business because they are not coachable.* They never go to a training class, or maybe they attend *one* and that's it. They feel they know all they need to succeed. This is such a shame. If this business were that simple, everyone would be earning a million a year! Everyone can, but most don't because they are not willing to be taught. They are not willing to accept that they need repetition. You cannot go to the gym one time and expect muscles. You cannot go to medical school for one day and become a doctor. You cannot take one swing lesson and hit a golf ball like Tiger

Woods. I have earned eight figures in my network marketing business, and I still attend basic training classes to keep my axe sharp. It helps me to shake off all the new ideas that don't work which came my way between trainings! This business is about the fundamentals. Keep getting trained.

Weekly training conference calls. Most every team in the industry has a team leader who conducts trainings by phone or online once or twice per week. This is extremely important and powerful. I have listened to two calls a week for 15 years as of the writing of this book. I credit so much of my personal growth and my income growth to these calls. My upline did a great job with these calls, but he also got great guest speakers on to spice it up and to give fresh perspectives on the usual topics. What also inspired me to no end was when rising stars on the team were asked to jump on and share their testimonials. When I heard some of my peers being recognized on a national call, I said, "Wow, if they can do it, so can I!" It motivated the heck out of me. I wanted to go out and create some success so I would be asked to share my story!

Find out when your team's weekly calls are, and get on them all. This is crucial; you *have* to get good at calling your downline and *promoting* for *them* to get on these calls, too. What good is it to be recruiting people into your business if they are not inspired, trained, and producing? Often, your downline will not listen to you, because they don't feel they can learn from someone who is not yet successful themselves. Or even if you are successful in the business, they can only hear from you so many times before they become deaf to your voice. A prophet is never welcomed in his own home town. They need to hear from fresh voices. And that is the beauty of being system dependent. You don't want their success to always hinge on you. As long as the conference calls and classrooms are there, your team will keep getting inspired and trained!

Attend your corporate convention. This is where everyone in the company comes together, usually once a year. These are often exciting, belief-building, and emotional. Conventions serve multiple purposes:

- Corporate roll-outs and announcements are made

- Learning from the top earners all in one weekend on one stage

- Getting together with your team from around the country and building relationships

- Giving you a benchmark or finish line to attach business goals to

- Recognition to all who achieved certain levels of success

- Time of reflection for yourself about your goals and progress

- Fun getaway / change of scenery.

The system is a proven formula. Do not try to reinvent the wheel. The wheel works just fine. The top earners in your business are using it very well. If you want the results and lifestyle they've got, just copy what they did to get there.

The following graphic is a great visual to always remember. Do not stray from The System, or get off track. The track is the proven way to success. It is the system your upline is using and getting lasting results. Your upline, maybe the top earner way above you, is likely sticking to the basics and keeping things simple. The experts do not engage in the idea-of-the-week. They stay focused and master the mundane. It works! It will keep working. They are on the track every day, and all you have to do is stay on that same track with them.

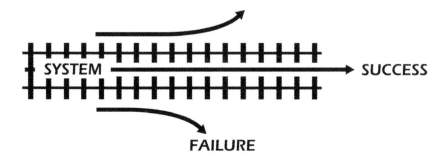

But often we see networkers think they have found or invented a better way. They are going to do it better, faster — and show their company how brilliant they are. Here's what I always told my team: "I am on this track right here. This is the proven path. If you decide to veer off to the right or left to pursue some shiny object or new approach, I will be right here on the track. I'm not going to follow you out to the side. We will still be here making money hand over fist, and will welcome you back when you are ready to plug back in."

Look, we are all entrepreneurs, and we're a creative bunch. That's what makes us entrepreneurs. We don't like to work for anyone else, or be told what to do. I had this creativity dilemma myself when I first got into network marketing. I wanted to apply things I learned in my real estate career to this model. My upline wisely said to me, "Brian, I know you are a brilliant marketer. And you have some great ideas. Some might actually be helpful. But this business is all about a System that will persist and duplicate before and after you. Let me just check, you do want to build a business that will grow even when you no longer are building it, right? OK, so what you must do is trust the system you bought into, and just use your creativity to get more people to *plug into it …* *instead of changing it.*"

This was *huge* for me to hear and grasp. So I took my excitement and used it to promote the proven System, rather than wasting my time trying to invent a new one. And because I did this, I got off to an insanely successful start and my business has flourished ever since for 15+ years.

This, my friends, is The System … the backbone of it. Everyone launches their business by getting excited, making their list, and hosting a PBR and a PCC. Then once those steps are complete, the *rhythm* of The System kicks in. The weekly briefings, trainings, and annual conventions are an ongoing machine that you just keep plugging yourself and your team into. But there are other activities that will *feed into* this system as well.

TOOLS AND EVENTS

Building your network will be driven by two things — *tools* and *events* — and your ability to promote and teach others to promote them.

The premise behind why tools and events are everything is that you are *always* to use *third-party* when recruiting or selling. In other words, always take the focus *off* of yourself. The goal is to aim the focus of your prospects onto a third-party tool or person — anything/anyone other than first party (you).

I decided that nobody was going to get more tools into peoples' hands than me and my team. So I stocked up on tools, and made sure my team was buying them at cost and cranking them out daily. I had cases of tools at my home office, in my car, and had them available at all events. I wasn't trying to make money by selling tools; I was trying to get them into the market in big quantities. This is a big reason why my team recruited thousands of people a month!

NETWORKER'S TIP

Whoever moves the most tools into the marketplace will make the most money!

Why is third-party a *must*? There are a few reasons. First, when you are new, you cannot possibly be effective at sharing the presentation properly. And your contacts *should not*, and will not, listen to your opinion about your opportunity because they know you are new and not an expert. So what The System calls for is for you to introduce your prospects to your upline expert whom you *edify* first. To *edify* means you speak very highly about this person in glowing terms, thereby giving that expert the *credibility* necessary for him/her to influence your prospect *for you*. Sometimes it may be a tool, such as a DVD or a webinar, which you will edify and promote. This works in the same manner. Your contacts are more apt to listen and be moved by a video that you endorse, more so than you pretending to be the expert.

Another reason to *always* use third-party is because it *duplicates*. Don't do what works ... do what duplicates! You may feel like you are capable and competent, and willing to go do the presentations yourself. Great ... but *don't*! It is awesome that you are a confident person, and we will help you exploit your confidence to make you a fortune, trust me. You can never make it about you and your skills/ability. This is because you may be so good that you recruit dozens of people all by yourself, but the reality is that those recruits will not be as talented or as confident as you, and they will try to do to others what you just did to recruit them. And they will fail! Your brilliance sets your team up for failure, and you don't even realize it. Only do what "a dud can do to recruit a stud." In other words, if an average 24-year-old person cannot use that method to recruit a 50-year-old business owner, then don't do it. The 24-year-old will not be effective with that high-caliber prospect because that prospect will not see a reason to listen to that "inexperienced kid." But watch this: If the "kid" edifies a DVD and gets the business owner to see a powerful, corporate-produced presentation, he's got a real shot at recruiting him.

The focus *must* be taken off the recruiter and placed onto a third-party tool or person. Another option the "kid" could have chosen is to edify his upline, and a physical presentation could have been made via a face-to-face meeting or on a conference call. The point here is that when every person in your downline team is empowered to be able to recruit "above their grade," you have the recipe for duplication and exponential growth. It has to work ... *and* it has to be able to be repeated by everyone on your team.

Tools and Events are *scalable*. Remember, your goal is to build a massive team to help you get an even more massive customer base. So your strategy must be able to grow beyond your reach. It must be able to duplicate away from you. *The magic growth happens when you get* a *large number* of *people, doing* a *few simple things consistently over* an *extended period* of *time*. Not only can everyone on your team hand out a DVD, but there is no limit to how many DVDs can be purchased and handed out. It is cheap and easy to do. Anyone can direct prospects to a website presentation. Events like business briefings are also scalable. You can get your whole team inviting people out to these hotel presentations, and you can always add chairs to the room or get a bigger venue. Conference calls can work for a small audience of 10, and just as well for 1,000.

What are some of the *tools* and *events* that funnel into the seven-step system I described above?

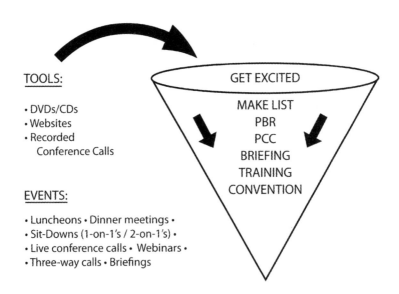

TOOLS:

• DVDs/CDs
• Websites
• Recorded
   Conference Calls

EVENTS:

• Luncheons • Dinner meetings •
• Sit-Downs (1-on-1's / 2-on-1's) •
• Live conference calls • Webinars •
• Three-way calls • Briefings

GET EXCITED

MAKE LIST
PBR
PCC
BRIEFING
TRAINING
CONVENTION

So, let's summarize how The System will flow. You sign up, get excited and make your list. You host a PBR at your home, and then a PCC by phone for those who cannot make it to the PBR. Now you have officially launched your business. From here, you step into the rhythm of daily activity of inviting prospects to a tool or event. You will use your upline (third-party) to help you sign them up at this point. Whether they joined yet or not, you funnel them into the weekly business briefing for a bigger picture. Then everyone will attend regular trainings and build towards the annual convention.

THREE-WAY CALLS

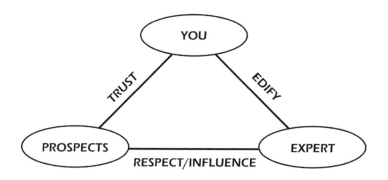

A major part of using *third-party* to ensure your business duplicates is doing three-way calls with your upline (or anyone you choose to edify). The first thing to learn is *how* to edify. Again, your goal is to bridge the gap of respect that exists between you and your prospects. As you look at the diagram below, understand that your contacts mostly love and trust you, but they do not *respect* your business opinion about this new venture of yours. So it is your goal to say things about the "expert" that will make him/her appear to be a much more knowledgeable source, and worthy of your prospect's time and attention. Your role here is to *take it off of you*! So you leverage your trust factor to *create* a bridge of respect between your prospects and your expert, and hand off the ball. *TRUST→EDIFY →RESPECT.*

Use this generic edification script as a basis, which you can modify slightly to personalize.

> *"Bill, I am glad you are interested. Now you know I am relatively new to this business. And because I respect your time and expect you would want you to get the most accurate and important information right from the best source, you should know that I am working directly with someone who is leading the national expansion of the company. He/she knows all of the facts about this, and knows how the big money is to be made here. You will love him/her; he/she is a fun person to work with — which you will see very quickly. But most importantly, he/she is so down-to-earth and just loves to help people. I am going to try really quickly to borrow just a few minutes of his/her time to pop on the phone with you to share some insights with you. Hold on one sec ..."*

Dial your expert, keep your prospect on hold until you reach the expert and upload your prospect's hot buttons to him/her. Then connect, introduce quickly, and *shut up*. Seriously. Never interrupt during the entire three-way call as your expert leads the conversation.

Before the three-way call occurs, determine the purpose for the call.

- **The *INVITE*** — You can use your expert to share their story and invite/confirm your prospect to attend an event (your PBR, a briefing, webinar, etc.)

- **The *CLOSE*** — Use your expert after a presentation is done to get questions answered and create urgency in signing up on the spot

- **The *MOVE-ALONG*** — Your expert can take a prospect who is not ready to make a decision and invite them to another event to see the bigger picture

- **The *WELCOME*** — If the prospect has just joined, they need to be introduced to their support team to hear success stories to reinforce their great decision

- **The *PROMOTION*** — Your upline can be used to convince your downline to do something (host their PBR, attend a convention, come to a briefing, dial into a team conference call, etc.)

Once the expert has done the three-way call for you, he/she should always edify you back to begin to establish *your* credibility with that prospect or downline.

Note to *EXPERTS*: You have been given the credibility and the chance to seal the deal. This is your time to shine. Do not get long-winded and go beyond a few minutes or else your downline will learn not to ever use you for three-ways again. (Ask your downline for honest feedback afterwards. If you do great, short, and powerful three-way calls, your team will have confidence in doing them and they will duplicate. *Duplication of three-way calls is crucial.* So stick to the "Expert's Agenda":

1. Share your background and your story about why you got started.

2. Mention the success you have already achieved.

3. Mention the many success stories across the whole company (use stories that the prospect can relate to, such as single mom prospect hearing about other moms earning lots from home and having freedom to spend their days with their kids).

4. Ask, "Are there any remaining questions, or are you ready to start creating success for yourself right away?" When answering, be brief.

5. Get the application started by directing them to sign up now with the team member. If not ready to sign up, move them along to the next step (an event, or further information).

6. Edify the team member so that you empower them to have some influence.

There is a direct correlation between the number of three-way calls on your team and the number of new recruits.

The more that take place, the more success you will experience. So I focus on promoting three-way calling activity all the time in my team calls and in trainings.

HIGH TECH MEETS HIGH TOUCH

If you ever research the history of network marketing back decades ago, you will notice some things have changed. But you will also find some things that work that will never change. The old-school approach to this business model used to be all belly-to-belly (high touch). Living room meetings (PBRs) and sit-downs (one-on-ones) was the epitome of our "word-of-mouth" industry. Then came hotel meetings (briefings). But networkers wanted to build faster and more efficiently. So fax-on-demand presentations, audiocassettes, and videotapes were created to do presentations without you being with your prospects. This brought a welcomed speed to the process.

Then a few decades later came the *Internet*! You could email website links to presentations and information, and the industry was abuzz! "No more meetings! No more face-to-face. A virtual business!" It took some networkers and even companies several years to learn the hard way — but high tech *will never replace* high touch. Technology can enhance the process and make some aspects more efficient like filling out an application online. Even hosting a webinar to present to people across the globe is an amazing benefit. But you will not succeed if you try to eliminate what created the network marketing profession in the first place — relationships!

Word-of-mouth works because it allows companies to market their products/services to our networks of people we interact with. Sure, social media is powerful and effective. But just as easily as someone joins your team because you grabbed their attention using Facebook or some high tech social media platform, they can be lured away to the next business by that same platform. Nothing can compare to what happens in your new recruit's head when he/she attends an event with a few hundred people who are all excited about that product/service/company. *Unless* you slow down and marry the high tech approach with high touch to create connections, you will only build a house of cards.

This is a *relationship* business. As a network builder, your team will only stay with you if they feel a connection with the leader and with their teammates. Get to know your recruits, their families, their goals and dreams. People don't care how much you know until they know how much you care. Be a servant leader for the team you want to build. Put their goals ahead of yours. Have you ever wondered why some distributors stay with a company for years without having much financial success? It is because they are getting more out of the experience than just income. There is value in being able to surround themselves with success-oriented, driven people. They enjoy the social aspect of making new friends. They love being part of a team and being part of a mission that is bigger than themselves.

You cannot put a price tag on the personal development and growth that people go through. Oftentimes, I have had people tell me that they look forward to the weekly briefing because it is more uplifting to them than going home to a stressful environment! Network marketing is about much more than money … so remember to focus on more than just the income aspect of this business. By being conscious of all of these factors, you will attract and retain so many more people on your team.

THREE RULES TO BUILDING YOUR TEAM

1. Exposure is everything

2. Fortune is in the immediate follow-up

3. Work with the willing

I learned that the top earners in network marketing were all recruiting-focused. Just selling the product/service is not going to give you exponential growth to your income. That is only created through leverage. My three rules of thumb have always been — *"Recruit, recruit, recruit ... and don't ever get them out of order!"* Recruiting is what will keep your income flowing in, even when you are no longer working. Would you rather be the real estate agent, only making money when you finally get a house sold, or would you rather be the broker, and get paid any time one of your agents sells a house? Of course, it's a silly question to ask a network marketer. But the truth is, many networkers do not truly grasp just how important recruiting really is. They often focus so much on their product, and not enough on the opportunity. Let's assume you know *why* you should recruit, but you are unclear how to recruit. Here are specifics to the three rules to building your team.

Exposure is Everything. You cannot recruit someone whom you have not approached. You must constantly be exposing new prospects to your opportunity, and add them to your pipeline or prospect list (your list should grow by the day). Exposing someone means you approach them to pique their interest in looking at your business. You'll invite the ones who are open and interested to any presentation type you choose, or the one that is most acceptable/possible for them (DVD, webinar, briefing, conference call, etc.). You should give yourself a goal of at least two Exposures per day. This is something that *everyone can* do. You will not build a huge team by focusing on activities that only the rare few super-producers can achieve. You must boil down the game plan to something that *every* distributor on your team can conceivably fit into their schedules. Can a full-timer expose 10-20 people a day? Sure. But 80-90 percent of your team will be comprised of part-timers. So in all of your team communication you should always address the plan for the team as a whole. What can even the busiest person squeeze into their day? I have found that two exposures a day is doable, and not so overwhelming that they would give up and not stick to it.

So what will your personal daily, weekly, and monthly exposure goal be?

Daily   _____
Weekly   _____
Monthly   _____

As the leader for your team, you must stick to your goal and do it! Then you have to *show* your team what you are doing and teach them to duplicate it. Ask for their commitment to doing so. Discuss their *why* for doing this business with them … then attach this activity to their *why* as the means to getting to their dreams. This will help them stay on track and do the work on those days they just don't feel like exposing anyone.

NETWORKER'S TIP

The magic happens in this business when you can get a large number of people doing a few simple activities consistently over an extended period of time.

The Fortune is in the Immediate Follow-up. I have watched so many networkers over the last decade who had no problem approaching people and getting exposures, but they seriously lacked in follow through. They just did not follow up. And here's what is so hard for me to grasp: *That's where you get paid!* You make no money approaching people. You get paid when you get them to see a presentation and then follow up afterwards to sign them up. Why bother contacting someone to look at your business, only to leave it at that. Ninety percent of the people I have signed up over the years did not contact me *after* the exposure to ask how to join. They would have just drifted away had I not called them (and called them, and called them) to get their decision and sponsor them.

I am proud to boast that I consider myself the "Follow-up King" in the industry. I don't convince, but I do follow up until they sign up — pleasantly and tactfully. I'm not over-the-top aggressive or annoying. As they say, "Amateurs convince, but professionals sort." I believe in sorting through large numbers of prospects to find the ambitious, interested ones. But I will also keep following up on sharp prospects who have not said yes, because I still believe they will see the light someday. My belief is that everyone I come across will someday be on my team. I feel this way because I believe in what I do *that* much. My belief is what wins people over. Yours will too. So increase your belief, and follow up until they sign up.

Find a *reason* or *excuse* to follow up with people. Maybe there is a new study just released. Maybe you have a new tool to share with them. Maybe you just had an exceptional earnings month, or won a company car, or saw someone in your company with your prospect's same background just retire from their job due to the business — and you want to spread the word.

Here is an example of frequency in my following up:

Day 1	Exposure
Day 2	Follow-up call to invite (to any action step)
Day 4	Follow-up call to invite
Day 7	Follow-up call to invite
Day 9	Presentation

Assuming they did not join at presentation

Day 10	Follow-up call to close
Day 14	Follow-up call to close
Day 30	Follow-up call to invite
Day 60	Follow-up call to invite
Day 120	Follow-up call to invite
Day 200	Follow-up call to invite

Each follow up will be a different angle. I might ask

what's new in their life (to see if a need for my business has arisen for them). I share a new success story to try to spark their fire. I will offer to put a new recruit I am about to sign under them if they join right now.

Do you have "call reluctance?" When your *why* is bigger than your *excuses* (fear, lazy, busy), then you will make the calls.

why ⟵⟶ **EXCUSES** or **WHY** ⟵⟶ excuses

Work With the Willing. As you recruit new people and your team is growing, whom do you spend your time working with? Only work with those who have the three mandatory ingredients for success — Burning Desire, Coachable, and *willing* to work. What you will find is that 80 percent will join and do absolutely *nothing*! When this happens you will get discouraged. But don't let it evolve into depression and paralyze you. It just is what it is. Move on! Recruit 100 to find 20 who will do something, and maybe one out of the 20 who will strive to become a star in the business. The point is, you cannot afford to waste your time with slackers. They will drag you down and hold you back. Work with the ones with big *why*'s who will follow The System right by your side. The rest can just plug into The System and they will call you occasionally for support. Do support them, make them feel loved, but you cannot direct much of your energy or time towards them.

RUNNING EFFECTIVE WEEKLY BRIEFINGS

The weekly briefings are a crucial component to building a team that will stick together and last long term. *People join for the money, but they stay for the relationships.* As discussed previously, the weekly briefing can serve many purposes. You go every week so you can learn the presentation, get re-sold on the vision, and bring prospects to hopefully join your team. Part of the reason for attending is for learning, part for socializing with your friends in the business, and part for recruiting. So the environment must be conducive to these goals. As a leader in your market, make sure your weekly briefing is striving to be *amazing*. You want your prospects to be attracted to join, and your existing team to look forward to coming back each week. The goal is for the audience to always be growing, and if done right, it will.

Here is a checklist:

❒ **Choose a nice hotel** — Your venue needs to reflect the image of your company. Do not select a dingy old hotel in a bad area, or a meeting room in an old building. Most hotels can get you a meeting room that will seat 30 people to start for around $100-$150. (As it grows, so will the cost … but so will the number of people contributing to cover it.)

❒ **Contribution** — Every distributor in the area who plugs in to utilize the briefing pays $10 to cover the cost (so one person does not bear the brunt of the cost.) As the meeting grows, you may have enough distributors attending to lower the cost to $5.

❒ **Sign-In Table** — This is the first impression of your business when your prospects or distributors walk up to the meeting room. So put your sharpest, nicest people at the table. They must be outgoing, polite, smiling and able to handle people who sometimes are not pleasant. These volunteers need to know how important this role is to the success of the meeting. When people sign in, give distributors one color name tag, and the guests another. This way everyone will know how to tailor their conversations when they meet.

❒ **Set Up** — Chairs should be set up theater style. Only set up half the number as you expect to show up. If you expect 30 attendees, set up 15 and put down more chairs only when needed. As you add chairs as people enter, this creates an air of excitement and the guests feel like there is more demand for this than was expected!

❒ **Music** — The room cannot sound silent like you are at a funeral. There needs to be upbeat, but professional, music that is pleasing to everyone. Not too loud, but just enough where it fills the room. I always remember Tina Turner's "Simply the Best" playing at many briefings I have done.

❒ **Introduction** — The people in the room need to be politely invited/asked to stay in their seats, turn off their phones, and then edify and introduce the speaker (60 seconds). Do not go long here!

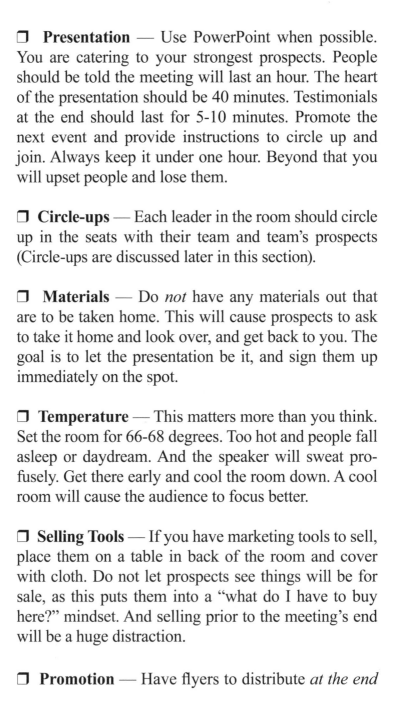

❏ **Presentation** — Use PowerPoint when possible. You are catering to your strongest prospects. People should be told the meeting will last an hour. The heart of the presentation should be 40 minutes. Testimonials at the end should last for 5-10 minutes. Promote the next event and provide instructions to circle up and join. Always keep it under one hour. Beyond that you will upset people and lose them.

❏ **Circle-ups** — Each leader in the room should circle up in the seats with their team and team's prospects (Circle-ups are discussed later in this section).

❏ **Materials** — Do *not* have any materials out that are to be taken home. This will cause prospects to ask to take it home and look over, and get back to you. The goal is to let the presentation be it, and sign them up immediately on the spot.

❏ **Temperature** — This matters more than you think. Set the room for 66-68 degrees. Too hot and people fall asleep or daydream. And the speaker will sweat profusely. Get there early and cool the room down. A cool room will cause the audience to focus better.

❏ **Selling Tools** — If you have marketing tools to sell, place them on a table in back of the room and cover with cloth. Do not let prospects see things will be for sale, as this puts them into a "what do I have to buy here?" mindset. And selling prior to the meeting's end will be a huge distraction.

❏ **Promotion** — Have flyers to distribute *at the end*

to promote the next briefing and the next training.

All of the activity of exposures and follow-ups through-out the week are leading up to getting people out to the week-ly briefing. So make sure you are always looking for ways to improve how it comes off. Hold a meeting with your meeting holders once a month or quarter for a *Plan-Do-Review*.

A note to all Meeting Holders:

Do not get so discouraged that you shut your briefing down if the attendance is not growing. I watched a leader on my team in Hawaii from afar, as he launched a briefing. Every week he would show up, set up, and conduct the one-hour presentation ... and sometimes the only person that was in the audience was his wife or maybe two other distributors. This went on like this for about nine months. But he held true to his vision of building a success briefing and business. Eventually he recruited a couple sharp guys, and it finally got traction and began to grow. About a year later, he was seeing over 150 people a week showing up. He soon found him-self making $20,000 a month. Who would have stuck around holding meetings that were costing him hundreds each night for nine months? He did ... and he won! The only way for your briefing to fail is to shut it down. Never concede! Just recruit more.

BRIEFING/MEETING ETIQUETTE

You spend so much time chasing your prospect down and you finally get him out to see a Business Briefing. He is a professional, or a business owner, and you hold him in high regard. But to your dismay, he is totally turned off by how people appear. Nobody is greeting him. He overhears gossip or negative chatter or whining. Some of the people are wearing jeans, shorts, or tennis shoes. The lack of professionalism is a real turnoff to him. During the presentation, phones are going off, people are getting up to get water, the speaker is losing her train of thought, and he loses his own focus. At the end, people scatter and so he assumes he should be leaving too, so he says he will get back to you about everything and leaves. This disaster can be avoided … it must be avoided if you wish to build a big team. Every team leader and meeting holder must teach on this topic at least once a month to his or her local team!

Here are some of the key points to focus on:

1. *Arrive 30 minutes prior to the start of the meeting.* The "Pre-Meeting" is the most important part. This is where your prospect can catch the energy from excited associates/distributors even before the actual Presentation begins. Give your prospect a glass of water and make them feel comfortable. It's amazing what holding a glass does to their comfort level. Remember when you went to a club, bar, or social event and had nothing in your hands?

2. *Bring only a positive attitude.* Leave your problems in the car. Talk only about how awesome this business is, how much money is being made, share success stories, and how it's changed your life.

No "shop talk" about lost applications, guests not showing up, or even questions about the business. Remember, everyone is listening!

3. *Contribute to room costs.* Distributors pay a fee to help pay for the high cost of renting a nice meeting room so we can have a place to bring our guests.

4. *Do not wait in the lobby for your guests.* This sends the message that you "need" them. You never want to appear desperate. Our guests should feel privileged to be invited. They can find the room (unless you are really recruiting down).

5. *Dress for success.* This is *your* multi-million dollar business. Dress your best. No jeans, sneakers, work boots, or hats. Make sure to inform your guests how to dress. Prospects need to see a picture of success. Business attire, or business casual, at a minimum.

6. *No kids.* Sorry, but this is a business meeting. Would you take your kids to a job interview? Of course not. Kids are too cute and they will steal the attention away from the speaker. No exceptions, including guests.

7. *No seat saving.* If you get there on time, you get the good seats. The best seats are up front. Don't sit in the back; this is where you experience the most distractions. If your guest sits in the back, he/she will be distracted by everything. Having empty

seats in the first five rows makes the whole meeting look bad. Get your guests up front, into the mix. No waving to your latecomers as they enter ... don't even watch the door. That is a huge distraction to all. Watch the presentation like it's your first time. No empty seats.

8. *Turn off cell phones.* This is a major distraction to the speaker, the guests, and the team. Just turn them off for one hour and encourage your guests to do the same before they enter the room. You don't want them to be embarrassed.

9. *Stay seated no matter what.* Never get up during the presentation. Not for water, the bathroom, or to greet your late guest ... never!

10. *No talking during the presentation.* You destroy the credibility of the speaker if you answer your prospect's questions during the presentation. It will also distract everyone else and may cause the speaker to lose focus.

11. *Participate.* If the associates in the seats are not laughing at the jokes, raising their hands when asked questions, and sitting forward, the speaker will struggle to create energy. This hurts your business. Contribute to the positive energy and watch your sign-up ratio go through the roof. Warning: Don't go overboard with participation and make it seem rehearsed. Be natural, but be involved.

12. *Stay seated for 60 seconds.* When the presentation is done, the music will come on immediately. At this time, stay seated with your guests for 60 seconds. Now simply turn to them and ask, "What did you like best about what you just heard?" Then, if the guest is interested, take them right to the front of the room to meet the speaker or circle up with your upline leaders. If they aren't interested at all, escort them out of the room right away so they don't spoil it for the positive folks.

13. *Use the speaker to close.* The person in front of the room who just spoke has the most credibility. Don't try and close your own friends or prospects. Get in line and take them to the speaker, this makes them feel special. When the speaker refers them back to you to sign up, make sure you have applications ready!

14. *Don't leave the room.* As soon as you leave the room and enter the hallway to sign up your guests …you lose. Now you are in convince mode and chances of them signing up is decreased by 50 percent. Stay in the room; it's your playing field where you stand strong on your turf.

15. *Always promote the next event.* The purpose of any event is to promote the next event. So as a team player, go around and talk up the next event. Encourage people to take flyers. If there are tickets, sell them. Treat the next event like it's the biggest and best event.

16. *Introduce your new recruit.* Make your new team member feel welcome by introducing them to others at the end of the meeting. Get your guests into the "circle-up" with your team.

17. *Testimonials.* If you are chosen to do a testimonial on stage during the presentation, stay within 30 seconds, maximum. Your job is not to convince, explain, or train ... it is to tell your story. Simply state your name, quick background, why you got into the business, and what it has done for you and your family/lifestyle. The goal is to connect with the crowd. You want them to say, "If he/she can do it, so can I." Please don't repeat the facts or tell them why they need to get started. This is not the time to spout off quotes, or to close or recap. You simply want to share how the business has solved a problem in your life so the guests can relate and say, "Wow, I want to do that, too!"

CIRCLE-UPS AFTER BRIEFINGS

Building culture is a very important aspect of our business. The circle-up is a great opportunity to build culture and get your new recruit started right at the end of every event. Your goal is to *inspire* and cause immediate action.

How to Begin Your Circle-up

1. Immediately gather chairs and place them in a circle.

2. Encourage your team members to quickly join the circle-up. Lollygagging kills the energy, so hurry!

3. Avoid leaving the meeting room because the circle-up may need your story.

4. Your circle-up should last 10 minutes.

Things to Discuss In Your Circle-up

1. Welcome guests/new recruits to the team/family (with assumptive posture) and initiate application process. Have them sign up right then.

2. Explain to them how they are a *part of the team.* They are in business for themselves, but not by themselves.

3. Promote First Step Document/Plan (your company should have a one-page document). Schedule PBRs/PCCs for new recruits. Have someone tell his or her quick PBR success story to inspire everyone.

4. Promote the next event. Encourage them to pick up flyers as they leave the room. If there are physical tickets available for the next event, they should be sold in your circle-up.

5. Share any new success stories or rank advancements with the circle.

6. Paint the Vision for what the team is going to ac-

complish and what this means to each person in the circle. Help them *believe* they will go to the top, and picture what life will be like when they do.

7. Promote use of tools. New associates get one chance to make a first impression so it's vital to use third-party tools in the exposure process. Warn them not to run out and explain anything themselves, but rather invite to their PBR/PCC, or if they insist, use a tool (DVD, website, etc.).

8. Suggest personal development (book, CD, etc.), to help inoculate them from negativity they may receive in the beginning of their business.

Your *posture, energy, and passion* need to shine during the circle-up. You are leading people, so show them who they are following. Leaders build circles, and then teach other to build circles.

3

Become a Builder

IPA — INCOME PRODUCING ACTIVITY

You know the term *time management*, right? Oh, what a misnomer. Who really believes they can manage or control time? Time is going to pass regardless of what we do. You cannot slow it down nor add hours to a day. We have no control over time … but we can control what we *do* with our time. Time management really is about scheduling our day to ensure we are being as productive as we want to be.

As we all know, business is not all there is to life. We have families/kids, meals, laundry, sports/gym, lawn care, grocery shopping, church, school, sleep, cleaning, bowling, movies, and somehow we have to fit in making money! Always remember this — in network marketing, you own your own business. This is a *business*! It must be treated like one in which you invested $100,000. If you choose to treat it as a little home based "program" that you meddle with, it will not succeed. At least it will not create huge income. You have got to sit down and think through the priorities in your life, and get your business to rank very high on this list. Determine how much time a day/week you will devote to building it. If you are part time, this may be an hour every evening and four hours on the weekends. If you are cranking it up and able to go full-time, then you should be working your business at least as many hours as you did your prior job/career.

Here's the rub. Most networkers *think* they are "working their business," when in fact 90 percent of their time is being spent on things that make *zero* money! The only activity that makes you money in this business is *income producing activity* (IPA). This is defined as time spent talking to a *prospect* (either yours or for someone in your downline). Everything else is considered "B activity." Some B activity has to be done, such as calling your team to promote for an event, checking emails, calling the company to order supplies, or checking on an application. But just know that this is not generating any income for you. Sadly, most of the typical networker's day is wasted doing this activity. So again, IPA is what you need to *consciously* focus on.

Let's diagnose your current situation. Take a look at this coming week and write down everything you do all day long. Include everything from eating, running errands, homework with the kids, exercise, social media, and whatever you spend time on for your business. Maybe in a given day your business activity was two hours (assume you are part-time). Out of that time, how much was engaged in dialogue with a prospect? Maybe 20 minutes? Do you feel you will build a six-figure income with that small amount of IPA? I have done this assessment with countless full-time networkers who claimed they were working their business eight hours a day. But after we broke down where their time was being spent and how much was real IPA, they discovered they were only talking to prospects maybe one hour of their day! What a wake-up call! Awareness is an amazing thing, as I watched some of them cut out so much B activity and start consciously using their time to actually make money by doing more presentations and follow up calls. Do more IPA, and teach your team to do more and watch your business suddenly explode!

SORTING THROUGH THE NUMBERS

Recruiting is a game of numbers. You will never know which prospect will be interested or not. Nor will you know which recruit will be a producer or a quitter. The game plan is to recruit everyone you can, and within 90 days they will sort themselves out. Some will be *studs* while most will be *duds*. I wish I had a device that would allow me to scan a prospect's forehead and tell me if they have a burning desire, will be coachable, and will be willing to work. But after looking around for this device, I have found it doesn't exist. Or maybe the top earners in the industry all bought them up and they were sold out when I went to get mine. Bottom line is that the more prospects you talk to, the more likely you will find some good recruits. And the more you practice at it, the more effective at recruiting you will become.

> *"You can never say the right thing to the wrong prospect, and you can never say the wrong thing to the right prospect."*

I agree with the first part of this industry quote ... if someone is closed-minded, you just can't do anything about that. And you don't need to; it's their loss! Some will, some won't. So what? Move on!

The second part of the quote is semi-true in my mind.

If someone is open and looking for an opportunity, you still need to do your best at trying to convey the information in an effective manner. The quote attempts to squelch the networker's fear of approaching prospects and messing it up. While I agree that there is nothing to fear, you still want to remember that third-party is always best. Not only will third-party have more credibility, but it will also duplicate when that new recruit approaches prospects. So all I am saying is stick to The System of *tools* and *events*, edify, and introduce to third-party. Do it with enthusiasm because the prospects are buying *your belief*!

Do you want to recruit someone you think may be a dud? Yes! First off, you can't judge a book by its cover. But more so, it's who *they* know that matters most anyway. You don't recruit *to* … you recruit *through*. A recruit is not the end game; better yet, he/she is a doorway to hundreds of contacts that otherwise you would not have met. So network *through* them to find the studs they can lead you to.

RECRUITING
THROUGH

I say "duds will lead you to studs" as I have watched this play out hundreds of times on my own team! Or "Links and Leaders" is another common term. Just keep the chain going until you find a leader. Look at a few real examples that occurred on my team. Starting with me at the top, you can see the progression of qualities of the next several people I recruited.

- Me	- Me
- Some Success	- Quitter
- Quitter	- $7 Million Earner
- Quitter	- $3 Million Earner
- Quitter	- Quitter
- Some Success	- Quitter
- Quitter x29	- $1 Million Earner
- Some Success	- Some Success
- Some Success	- $1 Million Earner
- Some Success	- $1 Million Earner
- $500K Earner	- *BOOM!*
- *BOOM!*	

Can you imagine how those quitters would feel if I tracked them down and showed them what some of the people they led me to have done, and how much override income they missed out on? Oh man, I would not want to ruin their lives by doing that, but wow I sure can imagine the regret they would feel! The moral of the story … you must *never* quit! And never stop networking through people before they quit so they can lead you to your next leader.

SORTING VS. CONVINCING

This is an important concept that *empowered* me to become the top recruiter in my company for years. I was once taught that "amateurs convince and professionals sort." And I lived by this daily. Stop spending so much time trying to convince people to do what they just don't want to do. If they are not open to an opportunity, move on and find the next person who is! Why beg someone to change his or her life with your amazing life-changing business? You don't need that person. Your business needs people ... just not *that* person. If they have to be convinced to join, you will have to convince them to work it and, chances are, they will likely not be coachable and follow The System. So just say "*Next!*"

Imagine you have a deck of playing cards. There are 52 cards, of which four are Aces. All you want to find are the Aces (holds pretty true to our ratio, in that out of 52 prospects you may recruit four decent potentials). Let's say I give you and another person each a deck, and I declare a race to see who is first to find four Aces. Ready, set, go! You flip over the first card and it's a 6. So you get your briefcase and pull out a stick of whiteout and a magic marker and begin trying to make the 6 look like an A. You spend minutes doing this only to find that the 6 will never be an Ace. Meanwhile, the "professional" sorter is quickly flipping card by card and coming across one Ace after the next until she finds all four within 20 seconds. The point is, stop wasting time on people who just aren't Aces! The Aces are out there, so just flip to the next prospect faster.

Now you *CAN* be a sorter, and still be good at following up. Convincers get stuck talking to the same four or five prospects and cannot see beyond them. Sorters with great follow up skills will keep finding new prospects to pique, while constantly circling back to old prospects to see if they are ready yet. If not, they put them back in the fridge to marinate some more.

OVERCOMING OBJECTIONS USING FEEL, FELT, FOUND

These are the magic words that you can use in every circumstance — to diffuse an objection OR to reinforce their positive observation. It takes you from a position of arguing your point against theirs, to a position of agreeing with them, which diffuses their concern and helps them see that they are on the same page *with* you. Now they feel they can trust your opinion as it resonates with their own. And likewise when they are expressing positive interest, you will relate with them and reinforce their insight and pending decision to join your business.

Here are some examples:

Objection: *"I've tried network marketing businesses before and it didn't work."*

Your Reply: "I know exactly how you *feel*, as a matter of fact I *felt* the same way since I tried some network marketing businesses before and failed, too. I thought I would never want to give building my own business another shot again after going through that. But what I *found* is that I was throwing the baby out with the bath water. After seeing how different this company's product and business system is, I realized that there were missing ingredients that kept me from succeeding in the past. This business is actually working for me! And I am sure you will notice the difference too and finally accomplish the reasons why you desired to have your own business back then in the first place."

Objection: *"This is another one of those pyramids, isn't it?"*

Your Reply: "I know exactly how you *feel*, I *felt* the same way when I first heard about this business and questioned its legitimacy. But what I *found* as I did some research was that this company has been written up in some of the most prestigious business journals, recognized by the Better Business Bureau, and has the backing of some pretty well known business entities. So that put to rest my questions about whether this was one of those pyramid deals that I have zero interest in! I'm glad you are looking to avoid some kind of scam too."

Positive Observation: *"I am interested in developing a residual income."*

Your Reply: "I know exactly how you *feel*, I *felt* the same way when I realized that getting paid over and over for something I did one time was possible. And what I *found* was that people in this company I am working with *ARE* receiving this residual income like clockwork, even when they are on vacation and not even working. I know I want that, as I imagine you do too. Let's get your application in and get after creating your residual income!"

You can *feel-felt-found* your way through *every* conceivable situation. Practice it until you find yourself doing it naturally on a regular basis.

Another way to overcome any objection is by disarming it with one powerful reply: "I'm sure glad you said that." Dave, the top earner in my company has used this line for years, and no wonder he has been so successful. He conducts himself in every conversation with a smile, probably because he knows that there is no objection that he cannot spin around with this one line.

As just one example, what is the hardest objection you could think of trying to overcome? How about this one:

Objection: *"I'm just flat-out not interested!"*

Your Reply: "I'm sure glad you said that, because this business is specifically designed for uninterested people! You see, even though you have no interest at all in what we do/offer, I can assure you that you know quite a few people who *ARE* interested that you can introduce me to. Now you can remain without interest all along the way, but I will teach some of those people how to market this business. And as they are generating revenues for our company, the company will keep sending all of these override checks to your home while you are sitting there being uninterested! So let's get you set up, point me to some people you know, and I will take it from there."

Objection: *"I just don't have the money to start."*

Your Reply: "I'm sure glad you said that. You see, lots of successful people in our business didn't have any money when they started. Here's what we do. You have no money, but you know some people who do. You introduce me to some of those people, and I will get them excited about this business. We will get them signed up and direct that commission to you, so now you have money!"

Objection: *"I don't have time for this."*

Answer: "I'm sure glad you said that. You see, lots of successful people in our business didn't have any time when they started. Here's what we do. You have no time, but you know some people who do. You introduce me to some of those people, and I will get them excited about this business. We will get them signed up, and teach them how to market this to all kinds of people you don't even know. As the override commissions are rolling in to you, I bet you can now afford to buy yourself some time freedom!"

CONTACTING AND INVITING

The name of the game is *contacting* new prospects and *inviting* them to presentations. This involves two different approaches: *direct* and *indirect*. And it involves three sorts of prospects we will call *reds*, *greens*, and *blues*.

Let's start off with the types of prospects, and pick the right form of approach for each.

BLUES — people who look up to you
GREENS — your peers
REDS — people you look up to

BLUES are the easiest to recruit. Because they respect you, you can pretty much use the *DIRECT* approach.

"John, you know that I am all about business and making money. I only play to win and I don't waste time on business ventures that won't make me money. I have come across a home run, and I want to let you in on it. Be at my house for a Private Business Reception on Tuesday at 7 p.m. so I can fill you in and get you in the game. See you there." (*DIRECT*)

Do you want Blues? Yes, because even if they aren't the most ambitious, they could be a link to some leaders.

GREENS are your peers who see themselves as being on the same socioeconomic level as you. And as we know, these friendly folks are often the most skeptical about taking our opinion about anything business-wise. So you can't just tell them they need to join you. You have to *relate* to them and connect *your why* with *their why*.

"Sandy, you know how I have been so stressed out for a while now about not making enough money and sinking deeper into debt? I have been getting advice from some of the most financially savvy people I know to come up with a plan to dig out and get into a better financial place. Do you feel where I'm coming from, and can you relate? Well, a very successful associate shared a business idea with me that looks like the way to change my situation. And because I thought you might be feeling the same as me, I wanted to let you in on this as well. Come with me to a reception he is having this Thursday at 7 p.m. and check into this project with me. It

might be the answer to our prayers." (INDIRECT)

REDS are more successful than you, and therefore most likely will not respect your business opinion about your network marketing business. You cannot approach them about showing them a way to make more money. They already out-earn you! So what can you teach them? With Reds, you must stroke their ego and ask for help.

"Mr. Smith, you know I have been keenly aware of your amazing success in business. I have admired your many accomplishments, and I often wish that I had a mentor to help me learn to be half as successful as you. I am really trying to find the right opportunity to create my path so I can be a great example and provider for my family. I ran across a business that looks to me like a huge opportunity. Since you know so much more about how to evaluate a business than I do, I wonder if you would invest an hour of your time to come with me to check it out (or invest five minutes of your time to review a short video) and give me your opinion. If you think it is a smart move or not a good idea, I trust that you would tell it to me straight. Would you do me this favor?" (INDIRECT)

Once the *RED* sees the presentation, listen to their opinion to see if they show signs of interest in joining themselves or at least becoming a customer. Do not let yourself get discouraged if a *RED* tells you not to waste your time on this business. This is just one prospect, and a clever approach. I have had *MANY REDS* tell me not to pursue this business simply because this is an unfamiliar business model to them. I still thanked them for their time. Now I out-earn and have more time freedom than every one of them!

In the recruiting approach process, it is always good to slow down and build rapport before jumping right out at them with your business opportunity (unless you are going with the sheer split-second-recruiting speed-numbers game, and getting prospects onto a sizzle call). Here is a very effective way to do this.

Ask the prospect, "What do you do right now for a living?"

Let them answer and show some interest, then ask, "What do you like *best* about your job/business?"

Let them answer and show some interest, then ask, "What do you like *least* about your job/business?"

Discuss, using *"feel-felt-found"* so they can see you can relate to them. Then say, "It sounds like you and I are driven by the same things, and even driven crazy by the same things! If the money was right, and you could have (quote the aspects they *like most* about their current job), and *not* have to deal with (quote the things they *like least*), and you could start off pursuing it totally on the side with little time commitment, I imagine you'd be like me and want to get all the info you can about such a company, right?"

What you have effectively done is asked them to *give you their hot buttons* to push. You will press on the nerve of the things that are painful to them, and flaunt the things they really enjoy. So they might say they love working with people and being creative, but they hate the long hours, rush hour commute, or having a cap on their income. Your goal is to use these items to see how your business is the perfect fit for them. They basically recruited themselves!

FLIP YOUR APPROACH / INVITATION PHILOSOPHY

If you simply reverse your thinking on how you will approach people about your business opportunity, the results will astonish you.

1. Don't find out who is interested in looking at a business, then expose them to the business.

2. Expose everyone to the business then find out who is interested.

Let's explore this and break it down into concrete numbers. If you start with a list of 100 prospects and ask who might be interested in looking at starting a side business, only 10 of them might be. Out of those 10, maybe five will actually go see a presentation. And out of those five, you might recruit two.

So it looks like this:
100 → 10 Interested → 5 Presentations → 2 Recruits

But under the flip option, what if you expose all 100 to the business without asking the interest question? Then after they have seen the business, they can know what to say yes or no to! Some may not allow you to show them or get them to a presentation, but far more will than if you simply ask if they are interested in a business they are unfamiliar with.

The flip option looks like this:
100 → 30 Presentations → 10 Recruits

FLIP YOUR APPROACH

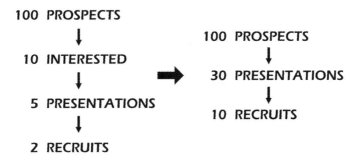

Here is another Flip philosophy:

1. Don't invite prospects to an event and then confirm that they can come.

2. Confirm they are free at that time, and once you have established they are free, then invite them to the event.

When trying to invite prospects out to attend a presentation (PBR in your home, weekly briefing, etc.), most people immediately jump into inviting them to the event at a particular date and time. What often happens is the prospect will reply that they are busy at that time. You gave them an out, and not knowing how great your business is, they often take the out!

So flip the flow of this around. Call that prospect and ask, "So Jim, what are you doing on Thursday at 7 p.m.?" Jim will say he has something planned, otherwise he will ask you why you are asking. You will again repeat your question, "Do you have plans at 7 p.m. that night?" If he is not tied down to anything, he will say, "Nothing planned, but why are you asking?" Now you have confirmed that Jim is free, taking that excuse off the table. At this point, you invite him to your presentation. As long as you do not say too much and give him cause to say he isn't interested, he will more than likely give you that open time slot and attend your event. After all, he has already indicated to you that he is available.

So don't invite and then confirm … rather, confirm they are free, *then* invite them.

F.O.R.M.

Don't make the mistake of trying to immediately jump right into your sales or recruiting pitch, ever! Your whole goal is to open a conversation to get to know that person and what makes them tick. As Bob Burg teaches, people will do business with people they *know, like* and *trust*. If you have not yet established this rapport, they will *not* buy from you or join your business, period. So let's get that clear now and forever.

So how do you begin this friendship-building conversation? Or maybe you are already friends. How do you begin a conversation that can *lead to* bringing up your product or business? We use F.O.R.M. This stands for Family, Occupation, Recreation, Money. These are four powerful conversation drivers that can lead to you discovering the hot buttons necessary to form a connection for you and your opportunity. So to begin the conversation, ask them about these topics. Then *listen*! They will tell you what is important to them. Listen for their heart and passion to see what motivates them, and *also* for any indication that they might feel a sense of pain due to not being able to fulfill some of these desires.

Family — Ask them about their kids. What do their kids like to do for fun? What sports do they play? How often do they get to do those things? Ask how they, as parents, enjoy time doing these activities with their kids. If they like to play soccer, mention how fun it must be to be cheering for them from the sidelines at their games. They might be at all of the games, or they might express their dismay about not having the time freedom to do so. Ask about where the kids go to school, public or private, or maybe what their plans are for college. Chat about the cost of tuition these days. Find out where their family lives and what they might do for a living.

Occupation — Ask about their career and what they like most about what they do for a living. Spend some time in this positive mode. Then follow up by asking what they like least about it. Insinuate that they are likely doing well in their career and feeling fulfilled because they are well-paid. Let them retort and bring it down from positive to negative, but you should never talk down about their job or income. Ask them what kind of demands their career places on them or if it requires travel or rush hour commutes.

Recreation — Ask what they enjoy doing when they are not working, i.e. hobbies, sports, exercise, camping, golf, fishing, bowling, working out, or taking vacations. Hone in on the ones you have in common and daydream together for a minute. Put smiles on their faces. Ask how often they engage in these activities. Ask what they would do if money were no object, and if they had the free time to go do it. Find out what they dream about, but might not have the freedom to act on.

Money — When you bring up money, it's never good to make them feel bad. Talk in general about the economy, about the prices of certain things, about the job market, and maybe about investments. Find common ground on what you agree on. Share how you have been thinking about how to plan for an early retirement, or how it feels that "enough" money never seems to be enough.

You now have a conversation going using one or more of these topics. Be sure to keep it 75 percent positive and happy. The 25 percent that might focus on negatives or *pain* they might have in their life will also come in handy when you introduce them to your opportunity. You will need to have and use *both*! Recruiting is successful when you *paint a picture*. You want to share with them how your business enables people to do the things they said they enjoyed, while at the same time ridding themselves of the stress of not having enough money for tuitions, or wondering how they will afford retirement, or feeling like they are on a never-ending treadmill chasing the dollar. In other words, it will give them all the things they value and want, and help them avoid all of the things they despise. Your business can help them create the ultimate lifestyle.

Once you have gotten here *without* even mentioning your business or company name, you are ready to unveil the business behind the curtain. You created curiosity and interest first. If you started right in with your pitch, you would have met with a closed door of receptivity. This personal restraint and patience is what the recruiting masters have practiced over and over. Bait the hook carefully before you attempt to catch the fish.

MIRROR AND MATCHING

It is important that your prospect can relate to you. If they can't, they are not likely to receive your message. Recruiting and team building is all about drawing people to-wards you and creating bonds. If you do not make them feel like they can relate to you, then you do the opposite and push them away. Your *tone*, *energy* and *personality* all play a vital part in this. If you are talking to a low-key personality and you are overly excited, you will not recruit that person. If you are talking to a high-energy person and you are too lax, you will lose them as well. So your goal is to subtly examine your prospect as you interact and try to best match them where they are.

Prospects all fit into one of *four* personality types.

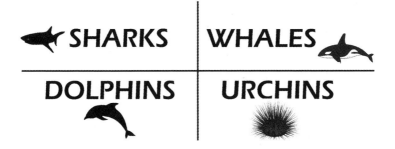

SHARKS — motivated by *money*
WHALES — focused on *helping others*
DOLPHINS — Social, like to *have fun*
URCHINS — detail, *fact* oriented

When beginning your conversation with each prospect, your goal is to use F.O.R.M. to find out where their motiva-tion lies. So you want to ask them a few brief questions about their Family, Occupation, Recreation, or Money. Then *listen*! They will tell you what is important to them and what their hot buttons are. You will get a sense for what personality type they are. And they might be more than one. They might be money motivated, yet also like to help people. In this case, your conversation should spend much of the time going over the comp plan, income examples, and how they plan to use this newfound money to help people they care about.

If you are talking to a dolphin, point out how much fun the events are. Show pictures of the company trips and talk about how much fun the people on the team are. Maybe you find yourself talking to an urchin who asks lots of analytical questions about the product, the company's financials or the comp plan. Load them up with the details they are looking for.

In every one of these cases, you try to be the best *matching* type to who they are … all the while leading them to a three-way call or personal meeting with a third-party up-line person who best relates to them. Birds of a feather flock together … so be a matchmaker!

RECRUIT UP!

Recruiting up means going after a higher caliber of prospect to have on your team. Most people do not recruit up … they recruit down. For example, you pull up to a gas station to fill up. You look to your right and there's someone with a new BMW, and to the left is an old hooptie. Which prospect would you opt to approach? *Most* networkers will approach the driver of the hooptie. They will rationalize it in their head that this person *needs* the opportunity more. While it may be true that the person needs money badly, it does not often bode well for your business. That person often doesn't have the start-up money, or ongoing funds to attend a meeting, buy tools, or even buy the product. You see if on a scale of 1 to 10 (in overall sharpness) you recruit a 5, what happens when that 5 recruits a 5? That makes that next person a 2.5 to you. When you recruit down, they will, in turn, recruit down. Soon you have a team of people who are not very sharp. *Why* do we tend to gravitate towards the person who is lower on the scale? We do it because we feel we will have influence over them. And while this may be true, the end result is not what we are after. So don't waste your time.

Ask yourself this when you are presented with a choice in whom to approach: "Which prospect will more likely become a leader and create a huge team under them?" Go talk to *that* person. You may not have natural influence. But that is *good*! You want to recruit people even more influential than yourself. They are the ones who will build your network/empire! Don't fear talking to them, but rather fear that you *don't* … and that someone else in your company does and earns a fortune in overrides because they pushed through the fear.

POSTURE AND CONFIDENCE

When you are contacting prospects, whether it's warm market friends or cold market strangers, you must come across as confident in yourself and what you are representing. If you *believe* in your product/service or your opportunity, then surely you should believe in yourself.

"But I am not good at sales."
"But I am not sure if people will listen to me."
"But I am afraid people might judge me."

"But what if they say no?"
"But I am not sure what to say."

You can "*but*" your way right out of the business if you let yourself think this way. You have the most amazing product/service you've ever seen! You have a company that is already paying people just like you six and seven figures a year! You have incredible tools and events that will present the information *for you*. All you have to do is tell a few stories and get them interested in checking things out. There is no need to fear rejection or not knowing all of the answers to people's questions, because all you need to say is "Watch this!" (and direct them to a company video). Anything beyond that you say, "Talk to him/her!" (and direct them to a call with your upline). That's it! You should have *huge confidence* for all of these reasons. You believe, and you are just looking for people who will see what you see. For those who don't, it's their loss! So have strong posture when you are engaging in conversation with people. Be real, be pleasant, but don't be a pushover, especially in recruiting. People only want to follow someone who knows where they are going and has *big vision / big goals*.

You will have ruts where you feel you can't catch a break. I've had weeks in a row when I could not recruit anyone. I began to get down on myself and questioned if I could do this. That's when you *must* call your most successful upline. Don't call your sponsor or just anyone who is not personally rocking the business — they cannot lift you from your funk. They will likely join on the pity party. Call the biggest star on your team and ask them to help you regain the vision and pump you back up. They will. My upline did this for me a few hundred times (seriously!). He likely hated taking my calls sometimes, but I bet his bank account smiled.

Always be working on your self-confidence and posture. Put yourself in your prospects' shoes and consider how your music sounds. If it is not upbeat, don't make the call until you change your music. Be sure to change it *that day* and don't let it go into the next. You cannot afford to go into a funk for more than a few hours. Listen to a great personal development CD in your car. Read *The Magic of Thinking Big* by David Schwartz or any book that uplifts you. Read stories of success on your company's website. There are plenty of ways to snap yourself back into good posture and a positive mindset. Just remember, this is *always* better than being stuck for the rest of your life in a job with no time/financial freedom.

YOUR STORY

Facts tell, but stories sell. We must always remember how powerful stories are. People will forget 90 percent of any facts you share with them by tomorrow, but they tend to remember compelling stories vividly (if told vividly). As a child, did your parents tell you bedtime facts, or bedtime stories? Story-telling is what network marketing is all about.

We tell stories about how we have used the product/service and what it did for us. We describe this with enthusiasm and in detail, which causes others to want to have the same experience. If we have not yet developed our own testimonial/story about what we are selling, we borrow other customers' stories and repeat them in the meantime. Both work! In recruiting, we tell stories about how a person retired from

her job because of her part-time income in this network marketing business. Or we tell a story about that person who just
got a new car paid for by the company. Or how you made X
amount of dollars in the business thus far.

Always put yourself into your prospect's shoes. What
do they need to hear that will turn them on so much that they
will want to join you? Meet them where they are. If you tell
someone who currently earns $35,000 a year working full-
time at their job that you earn $20,000 a month, you will
blow them out. Even if it is true (never lie about your income,
by the way), the concept of making that kind of money is
not palatable to them. At $35,000 a year, if you can merely
show them how quickly you made an extra $2,000 a month
in income on the side, *that* they could believe! They can see
themselves doing so to change their life! On the flip side,
what if you are trying to recruit someone who already makes
$100,000+ and your network marketing income is only
$1,000/month right now? This is where you must take it off
of you and use third-party. Edify and tell the stories of those
in your company who are making more than what your prospect earns. Then get them to talk to that person.

Stories, stories, stories. For recruiting and for selling.
You can even use stories to move your downline into action
by sharing success stories regarding the desired action. For
example, if you want your new recruit to host a PBR in their
home, you cannot just tell them what it is and expect that they
will excitedly do one. But if you share a few stories of some
people on the team who used PBRs to launch their businesses
and signed up several recruits in one night and made $500 or
$1,000 in an hour ... *that* will catch their attention! You see,
stories work.

My mentor told me that my first 30-day story was important, so I needed to create a great one. He said that if I can tell my prospects how much I made *and* how fast I made it, that story alone would make recruiting five times easier. On the other hand, if I made little or nothing in my first month, I would likely get defensive about it when my prospects ask how much I earned when I got started. I did not want to have to defend why I didn't make money by explaining that, "I did not take the business seriously when I joined." This is all too common, because, frankly, most networkers do not take it seriously right out of the blocks. They don't understand the importance and impact of having a *compelling story* to tell for the rest of their career.

Prospects want to know that they can make immediate money. So be ready to tell your story about how you did so. If you didn't create a great story back when you first started, give yourself one restart right now! Go start over and in the next 30 days, *make money*! Now you will be able to tell your prospect, "When I got started actually building this business, in a 30-day window, working part-time, I made an extra $800! And I can show you how!" Do you think this will work better than, "I haven't made much myself ... but you can"? Of course! It's time to use your great story more, or immediately go create a new/better one and begin recruiting with it like a machine.

YOUR 30-SECOND ELEVATOR PITCH

Every networker needs to have their quick 30-second infomercial on the tip of their tongue at all times. You never know when the next future top earner is going to step onto an elevator with you, or be behind you in line at the bank, or sitting next to you waiting for a table. You usually will not have much time to pique someone's interest and grab a new prospect. If you are not ready, you will often find yourself stalling trying to think up the perfect thing to say. And usually the person is long gone before you get up the nerve to open your mouth.

So you strike up a conversation by complimenting their shoes or tie, or their smile or car. Then you might ask them what they do professionally that has them driving such a car, dressing so well, or smiling so much. They will respond. Then comes your 30 seconds to pique their interest on your business. Here is one that I have used quite a bit:

> *"By the way, since you are so nice ... I actually work with the best paying company in America. We're a marketing/promotions company, and we market one of the most needed services/products in the country. Many people work with us on the side, part-time, and we set them up to make significant extra cash flow ... part-time. We are expanding fast and need more help right now in this area. Do you know someone with a great personality like yours who could use more income on the side?"*

If they say they are interested, now is not the time to go into presentation mode. Gladly take their number and tell them you will contact them to get them some info. *Do not* act all giddy or anxious to vomit details about your business all over them. This will scare the fish away from the hook. Just gently reel it in. Schedule a time to meet, or a way for them to see a presentation.

THE ART OF PROMOTING

Promoting is the essence of what we do in network marketing. We promote our product/service. We promote our opportunity. But we do these things by promoting tools and events. When we have a growing team under us, we promote certain activities and trainings (*The System*) to our team. When someone on the team feels like quitting, we promote their *why* for getting started in the first place to remind them why they need to stick it out and build. *Networkers are Promoters!*

Back around 1990, Mike Tyson was an unstoppable heavyweight-boxing champion. He was earning millions for every fight. He had raw talent, and people feared him. It was an amazing time in the world of boxing, as he was knocking out every challenger. People paid thousands just for a ticket to a fight, only to have the fight end by knockout in the first round! He earned many millions while he was fighting, but boxers can only take so much wear and tear. So eventually his career ended, and so did his earning potential. With poor financial management, he squandered most of his money and as of 2012 his estimated net worth was $1 Million.

Do you remember who Mike Tyson's promoter was? It was Don King, the man with the salt and peppered hair that stood straight up. He was known for getting into the ring after every fight to promote the next one. He stirred people's imaginations. He got people to think that the next challenger really stood a chance to beat Tyson. And they paid twice as much for a ticket to the next fight. And again and again, Don King showed his ability to promote. He promoted the fights, he promoted the fighters, and even promoted himself as the

NETWORKER'S TIP

Don't just hand out business cards or brochures. This rarely leads to sales or recruits. Your goal is to get *their* contact info ... you want to be in the driver's seat, not hoping for them to call you. Fortune is in the immediate follow up. You can't follow up if you gave them a card/ brochure without getting their number. We sign people up only by getting appointments.

greatest promoter of all time! He was just a perpetual promoter, and people bought into his enthusiasm. What's amazing is that Don King did not have boxing talent, nor did he ever have to take a punch. But according to Forbes magazine, as of 2009 his net worth was a reported $280 Million!

How does this relate to your network marketing business? It is precisely the same thing. You could become the top earner in your company if you just become the top promoter. You don't have to be the best presenter, trainer, or motivator. You just have to focus on promoting to a ton of people to go listen to the best presenters, trainers, and motivators in your company! *This is it, folks*! Become a master promoter. Take it off you, and put the emphasis and focus on the best in your company. Third-party is best, but the *best* third-party is even the "bestest!"

Remember that a part of The System is listening to weekly training calls conducted by the top leaders in your team? You want all of your team to be getting taught and inspired by the very best in the business, not just you. So every week my team has a call on Sunday and Wednesday evenings. Whether it's myself now that I am a million-dollar-a-year earner, or other top "Executive Directors," the best will be on these calls. So I will typically make about 30-40 calls to random downline people each Sunday and Wednesday afternoon *promoting* for them to get on the call. No, this will *not* make me any commission dollars from this activity directly … but indirectly when they are better trained and motivated, they do go on to produce more and create that override income. So phone promoting is very important.

Try not to call the same downline people every week. Mix it up, sometimes start calling from the bottom of your genealogy report and work your way up. After all, your leaders are hopefully getting on these calls themselves already. However, you will find that as time goes on, even many of them will slack off and start missing calls. When they do, by getting unplugged from The System, you will certainly see their income fall. So it makes sense to even call your leaders from time to time to ensure they are dialing in. They need to hear from other voices.

So what do you say to get a seemingly unmotivated distributor to dial into a call? Something like, "Hi Cindy, it's Brian, your upline [*top rank name*] in [*your company*]. I hope all is great with you! The reason I am calling is because there is an *incredible* speaker on tonight's call who will be teaching people how she was in a rut in her business, found a way to start signing people up, and suddenly — *BOOM* — her income took off! I know you had a big *why* for getting into this business when you started, but may have fallen into such a rut, too. That's why I *had* to call you urgently to let you know to dial in tonight to hear how you can blast off your business and income by copying what she's doing! Grab A Pen, let me give you the number again … "

PROMOTING EVENTS

Promoting events is one of the main things we do. Events sell, events recruit, events train our people, and events glue our teams together. We build our business from event to event. I don't do a PBR for my new recruit because I want to spend an evening signing up a few people and making a few hundred bucks in overrides. That's not worth it to me. The only reason I do a PBR for a new recruit is to book the next round of PBRs in the homes of the people we signed up. And the only reason I want to be in that round of PBRs is so we can book the next round. I build from PBR to PBR. And as I do them, I have my down-line protégé or aspiring leader there watching and learning. Then after a few, I let them do and I watch. Once I feel comfortable that they can do it on their own, I set them free to duplicate. I just set into motion a chain of *events* that will hopefully keep rippling out away from me … generating passive override commissions from living rooms I am no longer in.

NETWORKER'S TIP

Using third party is a sign of strength, not weakness. Weak people feel the need to prove they can do it alone. Strong people are willing to use The System and let someone else do what duplicates.

This goes the same with business briefings. The only reason I hold a briefing this Tuesday night is so that I can promote the one *next* Tuesday to everyone there. And next Tuesday, we will promote the following week's to be even bigger and better! How do you get the same people to come back again next week (and hopefully bring guests with them)? We *promote* the event as one that has never happened before, and will never happen again. "*This* is *the one you cannot miss!* It's never happened before, and won't happen again!" But won't next week's be basically the same? Yes and no. It will be a different speaker, maybe. Not all of the same people will be there. Some new people will show up. The exact presentation and insights will differ from any other, because it's live. And because everyone is excited and acting as if it will be a huge extravaganza, it gets talked into existence and now it truly has never happened exactly like that. So promote like Don King. Get people there. And then once they are there and that briefing concludes, *always* be *promoting* the very next event. We are in the business of moving people along from event to event. Never forget this.

"G.A.P." RECRUITING

GAP stands for <u>G</u>rab <u>A</u> <u>P</u>en. I would estimate that out of the 1,000+ people I personally recruited, hundreds of them came from *GAPing* them. Picture this: It was my first year in the business and I am sitting in my little house in Rockville, Maryland. It was the first house I ever bought back when I was 24 years old. Now I was 28, and I was still full-time in real estate still. I had also been in network marketing with another company for 3 ½ years, and my current one (second) for a year. I had just returned from my company convention after finding out that we were bought out and were now selling something totally different. I was shocked, but excited. I wasn't making much in the prior business anyway. So I was ready to give this network marketing industry one more run.

I told myself no messing around, this is my ticket, and I will succeed or die trying. I started recruiting and building like a maniac. My team caught traction and really grew from my energy.

I kicked out one roommate at a time until all four were gone, and I finally could live in my house all by myself (I rented out rooms to some friends to pay for my mortgage). I'm not sure why I am telling you about roommates, because even while they lived there, I was already doing what I am about to describe. But I just want you to get a vivid picture. I turned my master bedroom on the main level into my business "war center" (and I slept upstairs in a smaller bedroom). I had whiteboards on the walls drawing out maps of my downline. I had boxes of tools stacked like walls. I had my computer, fax machine, and my 900mhz cordless phone. That phone made me a millionaire! Here's how I used it every day.

My upline recorded a powerful 12-minute "sizzle call" about the opportunity. He nailed it. I believed in the message on the recording, and, therefore, I was effective at promoting it. So, in addition to using my Seven Step System, here's what I did for years.

I would call a prospect (either warm market or even purchased opportunity seeker leads) and it went like this:

"Hello Jeff, this is Brian Carruthers calling you from Rockville, Maryland. I understand that you are looking for information about working from home and building a business part-time so that maybe someday soon you can just work for yourself and have more income and time freedom. Now I can't explain the business myself over the phone right now as I am in a hurry, but Jeff, can you *grab* a *pen*? OK, great! Write down this number: (xxx) xxx-xxxx. When you call you will be able to listen to a brief but powerful 12-minute recorded message about the business. It will cover everything. Once you do so, we can talk. What time can you call the number? OK, great, I will expect to talk to you about 12 minutes after that time."

GAPing someone takes all of about two minutes or less! I would *GAP* about 10-20 a day when I was part-time, and then soon I was able to quit real estate and start doing 20-30 people a day.

Sometimes when I felt I had a strong prospect on the line, I didn't *GAP* him/her. Instead, the conversation went something like this:

"Hello Jeff, this is Brian Carruthers calling you from Rockville, Maryland. I understand that you are looking for information about working from home and building a business part-time so that maybe someday soon you can just work for yourself and have more income and time freedom. Do you have about 10 minutes for a brief overview of the company and the business? OK, great! Hold on one second … " At that point, I dialed the Sizzle Call number and flashed it into a three-way call. "Jeff, listen to this!"

At this point, I put the phone on mute, set it down, and started a timer/alarm for 12 minutes. I proceed into the kitchen to make a sandwich, or downstairs to throw in a load of laundry. When the alarm goes off, I grab the phone to hear the recording end, flash off the three-way call to drop the line, and say, "Jeff, I hope you heard that OK. What did you like best about what you just heard?" If his answer was that he liked anything he heard so far, I would use the *feel-felt-found* technique we discussed earlier, then got him on a three-way with my upline to close him. It worked so well. Still does.

Sometimes the person hung up during the call, so I would yell at the wall, get out my frustration for 10 seconds, and smile as I dialed up the next life I wanted to change!

After you have invited everyone you know to your PBR and PCC to launch your business, all the rest of your warm contact list should be called using this approach. And the interested ones will either sign up after the call, or if they want more information you invite them to attend a local event. Stick with your warm market first, but down the road you may want to add some cold market strategies to generate more prospects to talk to. This is a numbers game. Find a great Sizzle Call done by a top distributor in your company, and then crank through the numbers! This approach also works online by sending them to a website presentation.

WARM MARKET AND COLD MARKET

Warm market means people you know. This is where everyone should start. Your company chose the network marketing business model to get its product/service to the consumers because *word* of *mouth* is the most effective form of marketing. People buy the opinions or recommendations of their friends or family. When you want to go to the movies on a Friday night, what do you often do? You ask around to see which movie the people in your circle saw and liked best. We act on recommendations every day … from movies, to restaurants, to recipes, to hair stylists, to mechanics, to realtors, to vacation spots. When we make these recommendations to others, how great would it be if we got paid? Well, the business you are now in *is* such a scenario. If you *like* your product/service enough to use it and feel it brings you value, then hopefully you feel compelled and even responsible to share it with everyone you care about. If you ever recruit someone and they refuse to talk to their friends and family about your product or business, it is because they do not believe in it enough. Otherwise, if they *did* believe that it would truly benefit their warm market, they would be all about approaching every last one of them. A lack of belief is the bottom line. I felt so *strongly* about my service that I was signed up to market that I felt it was my *moral obligation* to tell everyone I cared about to get it! It was my *duty* to them. It is because I felt this way that I succeeded immediately.

"What if I have already burned through all of my warm market with other opportunities in the past?"

Get over it! We all make mistakes. You will just have to learn to humble yourself to them, and learn the right approach that will allow you to be received by them. Let's say you have gone to your friends/family about two other businesses in the last few years, and you are afraid they will run when they see you coming. There are two ways to overcome this speed bump. One is to just lead with the product/service and not the opportunity, and the other is a heavy dose of humility.

"Sam, have you ever heard about [your product/service]? Neither had I, until a friend just told me about it. I have been dealing with [state the problem that your product solves] for a long time, and it's amazing how it helped me out. You really should look into it yourself, I highly recommend it." Then pause and see if he bites and asks how to get info. If so, say something like, "I can get info for you, be sure to remind me. I will call my friend for you, I'm happy to help hook you up." If Sam doesn't bite, you can say, "I am sure it would be helpful for *you* too. Would you want me to have them get you some info on it?

This is where the humility part comes in.

"Sam, you know how I have been working insane hours, and struggling to figure out a way to create a better income while having more time with my family, right? Well you have watched me researching and testing different businesses over the years looking for the right one, as I have brought them to you to see if you were interested. I want to apologize if it seemed like I knew what I was doing and was trying to convince you to follow my lead. Obviously, I was not picking very good businesses, and I should have never approached you to get into them with me. For that I am sorry. I have quietly continued my quest to find a real business to be my solution. I was just introduced to some very successful people who are building a pretty unique company, and I believe it has real merit. But this time, I want to ask for your business opinion about it because I respect your insight. Would you mind taking a look and help me evaluate it since I cannot afford another misfire?"

The point here is that you should work your warm market first, not find excuses to avoid it. Where there is a will (a *why*), there is a way. Choose an approach, and go with confidence to get them in front of the information. Take it off of you and use third-party. For some you may use the Direct Approach, but many will require the Indirect Approach. So *what* do *you* do *after you have worked your warm market list thoroughly*? Well, let's assume you didn't just call each person on your warm list just once, but you actually did do ample follow-ups and tried different angles. You will actually follow up with them for however long it takes to enroll them.

From your list of 100 people, maybe you quickly recruited seven. What next? Network *through* those seven! Help them use The System. Get them excited, help them make their list, then host their PBR and PCC. Your goal is to turn their warm market into yours. Their goal is to get their contacts in front of you, or you in front of them.

If you truly learn to be a great networker, you can network level after level and never have to talk to a complete stranger. After all, who would you rather try to recruit — the sharpest people on your recruit's Top 10 list or 10 complete strangers on the street whose quality you know nothing about? Of course working your downline's list is always best and easiest. I have even taken the list from downline people who were quitting and called their contacts myself! I put the recruits under them if they didn't fully quit. Remember, work on become a better networker. Make your people's warm markets your own.

Cold market means people you don't know (yet). Is there a time and place to target cold market? Sure. After I ran through my own contact list a half a dozen times, I had a team to work with. I helped them approach and sell/recruit their lists. But I also wanted to stay in *Phase One*, which means in personal selling and recruiting mode, so I could lead my team by example. I wanted to keep finding some new recruits of my own, in addition to helping my downline recruit theirs. This way I could go wider while I was building depth. And I could have some control over my business success without having to solely rely on my current team to perform. So I added cold market methods to my game plan. This included the simple "Three-Foot Rule." I would try to approach at least a few people a day when I was out in public.

My goal was to make contact, pique their interest in a business, get their number, and give them a tool (DVD, etc). I tried to commit to doing at least two of these exposures a day.

Another way that I incorporated prospect generation was buying leads outright from a lead vendor. There are companies that do the advertising to find people looking to start a home-based business, and then sell those leads to networkers like us. For years I was buying about 100 leads a month, just enough so that I always had fresh people to call, while not too many that I couldn't call back several times until I connected with them. I built up a sizable database of these leads that I considered "my funnel." This allowed me to never be at a loss for someone to call. I dialed 20-40 people a day, as my full-time networking career was under way, and rolled like that for years.

The combination of warm market and cold market was a successful plan for me. My recruiting never slowed, my team kept growing (still is), and my seven-figure income is a result of sticking to this plan. I have stayed in Phase One since my first day. I enjoy it. I enjoy talking to new people. Most of the big earners in the industry get to a certain level and they stop doing what got them there. And often their business gets stuck at that point because they are no longer leading by the right example. They go into Management Mode, and their team begins to du-plicate this as well. The next thing they know, a decline in Phase One activity cascades down through the ranks and we all know what this means. Always stay in Phase One!

NEVER RUN OUT OF LEADS

"You are one recruit away from a financial explosion in your business!"

Have you heard this before? Here is what it means. When you recruit one person, that recruit has a list of 100 contacts that you would never have met. But now you get to connect with them through your new mutual contact. Your opportunity/goal is to network *through* this recruit's list of 100 to recruit, say, three people.

Guess what you now have? Three more lists of 100 prospects! That's 300 more people you can approach! From each of these three lists of 100, what if you only recruited on average another three? There's 900 more leads/prospects. Do this a few more times, and you will have more prospects than you will ever be able to call in the course of a calendar year!

If you realize that every recruit represents 100 leads, you simply need to start with your next recruit and *properly* work with them to share your company's message. In other words, don't recruit someone and drop them. If you don't work their list with them, then recruiting them was basically like you buying a lottery ticket hoping to get lucky ... and watch them go make you money on their own.

Here is a flowchart on how this will play out:

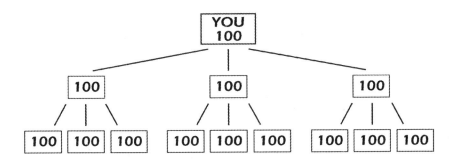

AUTOSHIP FOR CONSISTENCY

Getting on autoship for tools creates consistency in your business. My team was recruiting about 800-1,000 people a month. But then my top downline earner and I went into a studio and produced a great recruiting DVD so that every brand new and existing member of our team could easily use the presentation. Within three months of introducing this DVD, our numbers jumped to 2,000 recruits a month! Then, about a year later, the vendor set the DVD up on an Autoship program at $1 each with free shipping. Our numbers cranked within the next 6-12 months to more than 5,000 recruits a month! Why was the autoship component key? Most distributors will not consistently order and restock their tools. And even if they reorder, they often wait until they run out, and then have to wait a week or two for the next shipment. Meanwhile, they've killed their momentum. An autoship assures that you will have a constant flow of tools coming through your hands into the marketplace every month. When you get this consistency going with each person in your downline, now you can be assured that recruiting will be as close to being on autopilot as possible. My goal was to push autoship at every event, on every conference call, and in every conversation. Driving this idea exploded my team by more than 100,000 recruits within a short two-year period.

RECRUIT YOUR WEAKNESS

This is a tip that might help offset your own shortcomings, while at the same may be an effective recruiting tactic for you.

Let's say you have little money, but we know this business requires money for tools, websites, phone bill, attending events, buying leads, etc. This lack of money is the "weakness" gap you need to fill. So, go find someone with money and recruit them. Tell them that you have a huge opportunity to create an enormous income. Point out that they may not have much time for it, but you do. Tell them if they would be willing to join under you and help fund some marketing activity, you will spend *your time* that you *do* have (and they don't) to recruit people to put under them.

Your Weakness = Money   Your Strength = Time
Their Weakness = Time   Their Strength = Money

Maybe the flip scenario may be your reality. Maybe you have ample money to invest in the business activity, but you just don't have time to build it. So go find hungry, ambitious prospects who would love to build this business, and you help fund them. Note: I do not think it wise to get into a habit of using your money to do this often, as it is not very duplicatable.

Remember this: There is *always* an angle you can use to recruit someone. For example, your prospect says "I'm just not interested."

Your response: "I'm sure glad you said that. This business is perfectly designed for uninterested people. You see, even though you have no interest in doing this business, you would agree that you likely know a few people who are not as financially well off as you and would be very interested in this incredible business. So you simply introduce me to them, and I will get them started in the business and train them. Meanwhile, the company will keep sending you override checks to your home while you are sitting at home being uninterested. Sound good?"

GET INTO THE "NO FEAR ZONE"

Let's face it, we are not soldiers deployed in combat. We are not athletes getting ready to take a hit on the football field or in a boxing ring. We are not surfers attempting to ride a 20-foot wall of water that could crush us. We are business builders who make a living by showing people a business that can save/change their life! We have what they need! The challenge is that most people don't know they need it, and those who get good at conveying this effectively can get wealthy.

So what is there to fear in network marketing?

Fear of Rejection. What if someone tells you *no*? What will that do to you? Can we agree that someone informing you that they are not interested in joining your business will not do bodily harm to you? OK, so no physical harm is coming your way. So, it is the emotional punch in the gut that you fear. Nobody likes the feeling of being turned down or rejected. But this business is all about going through a game of large numbers, so how can you avoid the no's? The truth is you can't. The great news is that you can frame the no's so that it fuels you instead of upsetting you.

First of all, you are not asking them to marry you. If you were and they said no, they would be rejecting *you*. But in this case, you are asking them if they would like to join your business. Their no is being asserted towards the business itself, not you, the messenger. Always keep this in mind. Do you think a restaurant owner sits in his window watching the cars drive by all day crying because each passing car is rejecting the sign outside and the idea of stopping in to buy his food? No, they just weren't hungry. Or they just didn't care for his style of cuisine. But the owner still puts forth his best product and lets those who enjoy it indulge in his cooking. A few satisfied customers will multiply.

Every person who sells anything has to learn to take a *no* and move on to the next call/presentation. The key to success in selling/recruiting lies in your ability to go from *no* to *no* without losing your enthusiasm. Remember that we are in the people attraction business. So we must keep our level of passion and excitement high as we sort through the prospects because part of what they are buying into is our "*music*" — our conviction and attitude about what we are a part of. It's not *what* you say; it's *how* it sounds that is most important. Don't worry about having the right words ... that is secondary.

Have you ever fallen in love with a song on the radio that got you so fired up, yet you didn't even understand the lyrics? You even found yourself mumbling over the words you had no clue about while you sang it out loud! That's what we are talking about here. It's not the words that matter most. If you are excited, they will want to do what you do. If you are fearful, worried, and nervous, they will not want to do what you do. So be *confident* and excited, knowing that you have something they need. Your business can change their life. And if they don't see that, it's *their loss*! I always reminded myself that *no* simply meant "*Not now*, try again later."

Fear of Looking Foolish. Are you worried that you might not explain the information as well as some of the pros? Just remember, you know 100 percent more than your prospect knows about your business. So if you share the facts with conviction, they will buy in. If you are going to mess up the details, do it with pizzazz and confidence! And, of course, use third-party tools so that the facts will always be right on point, regardless. And if you don't know answers to questions, tell them you aren't supposed to be the one who provides answers. You are supposed to introduce them to the company expert (using a three-way call), or simply usher them to where they can find the answers (such as your website or upline).

Maybe you fear someone judging you, or making fun of you for starting a network marketing business. You will likely hear the word "pyramid" a few hundred times over the coming years. It's OK. Don't let their business ignorance affect your mood. I used to let that get to me in the beginning. But several years and millions of dollars later, I can look at people who say that and smile knowing that I out-earn and out-fun them doing what they don't understand. You are not foolish going against the grain. The real fools are the ones stuck in the grain of mediocrity.

Fear of Success. This fear is one most people don't know they have, but many people have it. You say you want success. You want the homes, cars, boats, travel, shoes, clothes, and lifestyle. But if you achieve all of that, how will your friends perceive you? Are you afraid of what your friends and family are going to think when suddenly your life changes and theirs is still the same? Right now, you are likely on the same socioeconomic level with them. It's comfortable and you all can relate to each other. It's akin to "misery loves company." But you go off and become successful in your new business, and —*wham*! You are now driving a nicer car or moving into a nicer neighborhood. You take your kids out of the public school with their kids and put them into a private school. You now take expensive trips, but your friends can't afford to go with you. Now you start to sense a separation or divide. You are moving up, and they are choosing to stay stuck. You are up here, and they are down there. Your friends are looking at you with a bit of jealousy. Knowing this can happen, what are you going to do? Are you going to go for it and succeed anyway, or are you going to stay small with them so you don't make them feel inadequate?

You may have read this quote before from the book *A Return to Love* by Marianne Williamson.

> *"Our deepest fear is not that we are inadequate. Our deepest fear is that we are powerful beyond measure. It is our light, not our darkness that most frightens us. We ask ourselves, 'Who am I to be brilliant, gorgeous, talented, fabulous?' Actually, who are you not to be? You are a child of God. Your playing small does not serve the world. There is nothing enlightened about shrinking so that other people won't feel insecure around you. We are all meant to shine, as children do. We were born to make manifest the glory of God that is within us. It's not just in some of us; it's in everyone. And as we let our own light shine, we unconsciously give other people permission to do the same. As we are liberated from our own fear, our presence automatically liberates others."*

Networkers who want success must develop a *no fear* attitude! It is only through the no's we will find the *yes*. You cannot avoid rejection, but you can look past it. You cannot avoid being bad at the business before doing the activities enough to become good. You cannot help that most of your friends will choose to be complacent and stubborn while they watch you soar into a new lifestyle. The *No Fear Zone* is where you need to live. You know where you are going ... so charge forward bravely and boldly!

SOCIAL MEDIA

Social media has become a mainstay in our network marketing world. There are some amazing ways to harness the power of social media to expand your empire. But there are also many ways to misuse the tool and inadvertently damage the progress you were otherwise striving for. Therefore, your web presence must be thought out and designed with intention and purpose.

We all get to project online who we are to the outside world. We can put ourselves in the best possible light, and present ourselves as we *want people to see us*. If you think about what would attract people to a network marketing business, that is what they need to see when viewing our online profile. Remember, people are buying into *us* before they buy into the company we are with.

I think about what attracted me to network marketing. Of course it was the income potential, so I need to project financial success. Nobody wants to be sponsored by a dud. I also liked the personal development aspect. So I talk about the growth and development I have found in this profession, and the books I have read. This seems to create some connection with those who might have also read those same books. The social part of the business was also very appealing to me. The networkers I had met seemed to be so happy, always having fun, and had such close relationships. So again, I want to project this out there so that it will resonate with people. I want people to say, "Wow, I want to be like him, live like him, and have what this guy has. I wonder if I can find out how he does it." So our profiles are like a billboard to attract people to us. We are in the people attraction business.

Social media is also a great way to reach outward to connect with new prospects you want to introduce to your business. Using Facebook, LinkedIn or other platforms to re-connect with past classmates or coworkers, — or even establishing new contacts in your target market — is very effective. All of us fell out of touch with people we went to school with and no longer have their contact information. But these days we can do a search for their name on the Internet, and we can also seek out a mutual connection and find them that way.

I believe that social media is a means of *connection*, not so much for *advertising*. If you are on Facebook, and you are constantly posting ads for your product or business, you might find that you turn off many people who otherwise might have been great prospects for you. Imagine if you picked up a magazine and 90 percent of it was ads. I imagine you would drop it and never buy a future issue. In the same fashion, nobody wants to see your social media presence as nothing more than a perpetual "pitch-fest." People want to see posts with content that is interesting to them. So I suggest you post things that you feel represent you and your interests, and frame them in a way that captures the minds and hearts of your viewers. It's all about creating *curiosity* and starting conversations. A natural opportunity will present itself later to share your business or product. So stop advertising and start connecting.

When trying to recruit using social media, I find that it is best to saying nothing about your business, but rather show the *lifestyle results of* the business. For example, I post pictures for vacations I recently took (because of my business affording me the time freedom and finances to take them). I choose not to even subtly remark about how my business made the trips possible. I just post about the trip, and let people comment about how lucky I am. Then in private conversation, I ask them if they travel much and where they would like to go next. If they divulge to me that they can't afford such luxury, I can give credit for my trips to the freedom due to my side business. I will do this in a way where I do *not* immediately ask them if they are interested in my business for themselves. As a matter of fact, I make no such approach. I await their curiosity and questions. If it doesn't come on this interaction, it will surely come after the next trip. Or maybe they will see me post about going on field trips with my son. Or pictures of getting a new car. Or pictures of spending time at a charity function. My whole goal is to engage people. Once they learn more about me and I learn more about them, the connection will soon foster opportunities for me to broach the subject about working together in my business.

Social media is also a way to constantly keep your team in the loop and inspire them with a constant flow of success stories to inspire them. For example, on Facebook you can make congratulatory posts every time someone on the team achieves a rank advancement, earns a bonus, or hits a goal. This not only makes the achiever feel great with public recognition, but it also inspires all onlookers to want to kick it into gear to achieve more themselves. People will work for money, but will die for recognition. When they see their name or picture on the screen from the worldwide web, they feel empowered. Their self-confidence increases and activity increase often follows. They will want to earn the next round of recognition.

If you go trolling the social media websites out there, be sure that you are not acting like a hunter. Don't message someone you see right off the bat with a sales or recruiting pitch. It is best that you find something you have in common to engage them in conversation first. Maybe ask them a question about their post or some advice from their standpoint of expertise on a subject. Paying them a compliment about one of their posts that you read will make them feel good, and thus increases the likelihood of them feeling a connection with you. Then, after you have developed some level of rapport, you can lead the conversation to finding out some reasons why your product or opportunity might benefit them. But if they sense that your sole purpose from the get-go was to pitch them, they will run from you. I find that those who genuinely *like* people, and are really interested in them, do well in recruiting. But those who are only looking to make a sale or sign a recruit, and couldn't care less about the person, often end up with no recruits and quit the profession.

Be careful not to alienate any viewers by posting messages that could offend them. It is wise not to mix politics and religion with your social media identity unless you are OK with eliminating half of the world audience. And remember, once you post something online, you cannot get it back. It's out there forever if someone wants to grab it and use it, for or against you. So if you want to be seen by your prospects as professional and someone who is ideal to do business with, do you really want to post that picture of you acting like a fool at the party last week? You can, and should, show your fun side, but I suggest that you think three times before posting. Always ask yourself, "Will my post add to, or take away from, my personal image?"

My final social media tip is this: Do not let yourself get sucked into your phone or computer screen and think that you are building an empire. Yes, social media is a great tool. But it will *never* replace personal conversations in person or by phone. That is where true emotions and relationships are formed and nurtured. The Internet is often a brain- and time-sucking device. Hours can go by, then days go by, and your business is not being built. If you are using social media, be sure you know why you are on. If you are just scanning for fun and social reasons, fine, but be aware of how much time you are spending on that. If you say it is for prospecting, then be intentional and productive. Create at least one new friendship a day. Every month you can add 30 new people to your friend network, which will soon translate into your downline network!

4

Harness the Power of The Model

THE MAGIC OF RECRUITING AND EXPONENTIAL GROWTH

As you see in this chart, we compare what the next five years can look like. At your *JOB*, you have *one* person making you money in the first year. But in network marketing, we expect

Years	J.O.B.	Network Marketing
1	1	5
2	1	25
3	1	125
4	1	625
5	1	3125

that you can recruit five people who will generate override income for you. In the second year, it's still just you at the job. But in your network marketing business those first five recruited five each. So now you have 25 more people on your team, making you money. Taking this projection out over five years, you will always have just *one* person (you) generating your income. But your network marketing business would have 3,125 people on your team by then! What if each of them made *one* sale next month?

Keep in mind that you will need to recruit more than five people to find five who will be actively in the game producing. And many builders will find *far more* than five producers per year.

THE POWER OF ONE (MORE)

MONTHS	EVERYONE RECRUITS 1/MONTH	EVERYONE RECRUITS 2/MONTH
1	2	3
2	4	9
3	8	27
4	16	81
5	32	243
6	64	729
7	128	2,187
8	256	6,561
9	512	19,683
10	1,024	59,049
11	2,048	177,147
12	4,096	531,441

As you can see, each person on your team recruiting just one new person a month can add up to 4,096 people in one year! But, if everyone agreed to recruit *just one more* each month, you would have over a *half million* people on your team … just by going from one to two recruits a month! That truly demonstrates the Power of *One More* recruit.

BUILDING DEPTH FOR STRENGTH AND SYNERGY

There is an age-old debate as to whether you should build wide or build deep — assuming your comp plan allows you this choice. There are some plans that are binary meaning you only get two legs. There are some that use a forced matrix and dictate where people go (i.e., the 3x3 matrix). But many long-lasting comp plans use some form of a "unilevel" model, which allows you to "go wide." This means you can sponsor as many frontline recruits as you wish. The depth of your comp plan will vary — some paying down only a certain number of levels (often 6-10), while others to unlimited levels if using a "differential spread" model. Of course, you will have to fit the philosophy I am about to explain into your specific comp plan. If you agree with my philosophy, which I think you will, then do your best to find a way to employ it to the best-case scenario in your company.

The key question I always ask is: Would you rather have 20 people on your frontline earning $500 a month, or have 4 people on your frontline making $5,000 each? Let's even assume that being 20 wide would put a bigger override per sale into your pocket due to the sales not being buried deep down in those legs. The problem is that when someone is only making $500/month, they could quit the business at any time. So would you rather have 20 spinning plates like a circus clown trying to keep them all spinning (in the business), or have four people who are making their full-time living from the business and are locked in and solid? The wider you go, the more you will have to worry about people not having enough momentum and support and quitting on you.

So remember what your *end game* is. I would assume your aim is to build a business that you can soon put on autopilot and have leaders running their own teams — and the overrides flowing up to you forever! You don't want to build yourself a job where you are always stressed out trying to keep everyone from quitting because they are barely making any money. This is why when you build *deep* under people, *fear* of *loss* is employed and it keeps the entire upline in the game. Who would quit on a business when they see all kinds of recruiting and selling happening on their team? In my company, we have the *CEO* send out an automated email message notifying everyone in the upline every time a new recruit joins somewhere in their downline. This serves as a constant reminder that their business is growing (often in spite of them). Because people will fear quitting and missing out on how big their business might keep growing to in the future, depth is a huge factor in keeping down distributor attrition.

Digging further into the philosophy of building down/deep, there are several key benefits. It is often said "a recruit is not a recruit until he/she has recruited someone." This is crucial! The business goes from theory to reality when they recruit someone. This shows them that other people do agree that this is a great business idea. They see their business starting to grow, going from only them to now two. And their first recruit needs a recruit for *that* person to feel this way. As the upline leader, your number one goal is to see to it that every recruit gets their first recruit *fast* (before they begin to doubt or even quit). It's all about locking your recruits in, and building a "leg" through them.

There are two ways you can build a leg down. You can drive depth in each leg by "taprooting." This means that you recruit Mary, and you help Mary recruit her friend John. Then *you* work with Mary to help John to recruit Tracy. Then *you* work with Tracy to recruit Cindy. Then *you* work with Cindy to recruit Chuck. And you will continue doing this until you find someone who truly desires "to be the *next you*" … a leader/builder (see diagram). In this case, Chuck turns out to be a stud! He catches fire and starts running to learn how to recruit, build, sell, etc. Chuck is on the prowl to take the baton out of your hands and soon run his team for himself. That's what you are always looking for!

BUILDING DEPTH

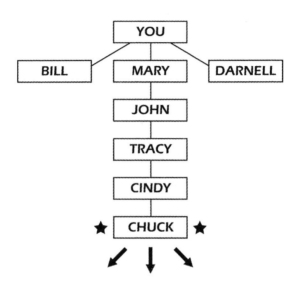

So you found a leader. Is that where you stop? No! A leader is not a solid leader until he has two more leaders under him. In other words, a leg is not "done" or solid until there are three leaders in that line/leg. You want to have over-lapping leadership. Why? Well, what if the leg has just one leader, and that person gets sick or decides to go do something else? The team might fall apart. Everything hinges on leadership. What if some of the people on that team don't vibe well with their one upline leader? Or what if the leader is on an airplane and cannot take an important three-way call? These are all reasons why having multiple upline leaders is important.

Think of the root system of a tree. If you follow the

main root from the tree trunk down into the soil, you will find a main root with many offshoots. The offshoots are extensions of the root in search of water and nutrients. The upline leadership (the tree) should always be following this same path down the taproot and following the offshoots. In networking, the offshoots are your people's leads/contacts. Trees have networks of roots, and network marketers have networks of distributors. As a leader/builder, your business needs new people just like a tree needs water from the ground. Often, a tree's roots must keep growing deeper and spreading out wider as it goes to find its sustenance.

Here is a good question that depicts the value of taprooting through your team. Would you rather talk to a new recruit's Top 10 sharpest prospects whom they can vouch for as being ambitious, or talk to 10 complete strangers who you have no way of knowing if they possess any good qualities? There is no possible way you will disagree with my view on this. Of course I would rather my new recruit introduce me to her Top 10 list! This way I am assured to have *quality* prospects whom I can approach in a warm market way. Either she will make an actual introduction (preferable, of course) or I can call her list and mention her name. It is always your first choice to have your recruit introduce you physically, or at least by phone, to her contacts. This is how you not only get the best recruiting results, but your goal is to *TRAIN* your recruit in the process. It's field training!

But if you have a scenario where the recruit is just not willing to make the introductions and is letting their list remain untouched, call them yourself! Here's a sample script:

"Hello Mike, my name is Brian Carruthers. I was referred to you by Nancy. Sorry if I caught you off guard. Real

quick, she said you're a successful sharp person and I was wondering if you're open at all to earning a residual income outside of your current career. If not I will let you go right now, otherwise, I would love to give you a website that you can check out and take a look at what we are doing."

"Well, what are *you doing?"*

"We're a half-billion-dollar company that's A+ rated with the Better Business Bureau [insert and use whatever credibility points your company has]. *Nancy thought this would be right up your alley since you are an entrepreneur on the lookout for new trends. You have a pen? Go to _____. There's a 10-minute video presentation from one of our company leaders. He's a million-dollar earner as well. Check it out and if you're open at all I would love to hear back from you. I'll give you my direct number, its xxx-xxx-xxxx. Thanks, Mike."*

That's how you drive down a leg and taproot. We are networkers … so network! But just as you drive this attention *down* the leg, you also want to bounce off a leader and take it *back up* that leg as well. A *huge* benefit to building depth like this is what Chuck does to each of his upline. Knowing that they override this big builder, they will often stay in the game even if they are not actively working the business themselves. What I do in this case is call everyone above Chuck and say:

"Hi Bill, it's Brian with another update on your business. You know how you led me to John and he joined? Well, John led me to Tracy, and Tracy recruited Cindy. I asked Cindy who she knew that was very ambitious, and she introduced me to Chuck. Bill, let me tell you, Chuck is on fire! *He has already signed up 24 people and is building a huge business. If*

you want to capture some serious override money from all of those sales, we just need to get a few more personal recruits for you so you will qualify to receive that money. Who else can you introduce me to right away?"

You burn a house the fastest by lighting a fire in the basement — burn it from the bottom up. If Bill on your front-line was the one who caught fire, the only person that would be motivated and excited by that is *you*. But if Chuck on the fifth level down catches fire, all four of the people between you and Chuck get motivated. The deeper the action, the more people it will motivate.

RECRUIT TO INVITE VS. INVITE TO RECRUIT

When you have a recruiting event coming up next Saturday, you invite prospects to come out to it. You know if they show up, they will likely sign up. So if you invite five in order to get one to show up (since the normal show up rate is 20 percent of those who commit to come), what is your best outcome? One guest can get you one recruit. This is called "inviting to recruit" (meaning you invited prospects to an event to recruit them). That is good, but not great. How do big builders operate to get bigger momentum?

"Recruiting to invite" is far more powerful and effective. Instead of inviting all week long hoping to get people to show up Saturday and only being able to convert those few … what if you use your tools (website, sizzle calls, webinar) or more immediate events (sit-down at Starbucks, weekly briefing, PBR) to *recruit them now* ahead of time? And now that they are in the business, they can make their list and invite all of their prospects to that big Saturday event.

So compare the difference: You personally invite to get one prospect to Saturday's event, hoping to recruit *one*. Or, you invite that person early in the week and help him invite 20-30 people from his fresh, untapped list to attend on Saturday. And if four to six people show up, your potential for new recruits that day went from one to six! What I have learned and practiced is not to put off recruiting by inviting to an event that is several days or more away, but rather recruit the prospect immediately so we can hit their lists and bring a flood of prospects to the big event. Remember, big events only happen every so often, so we must build into them far in advance by creating a groundswell of new recruits on the local team prior to.

RECRUIT TO INVITE

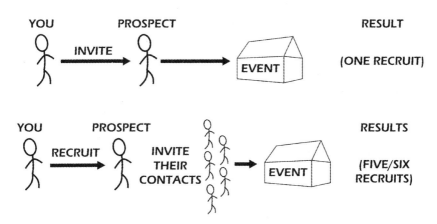

In order words, if you have a weekly briefing, don't lose the days in between. If you have a Thursday briefing and it is Monday, I would not invite people to Thursday. I would use tools to expose and recruit them on Monday, Tuesday, and Wednesday with the intent to recruit them *and* invite their contacts to Thursday. This way you are not getting production only one day a week, but every day.

A final thought relating to this topic is "Recruiting to" vs. "Recruiting through."

"Recruiting to" someone means your goal is to get to that person and recruit him/her. That recruit is your main goal or target. What I prefer to do is to "recruit through" that person. I do not get excited about that recruit, but rather all of the vast resources of prospects they can lead me to. One person does not move your business results, but a leader you can sell and recruit large numbers through *does*. So the only reason we want to recruit someone is so that we can recruit everyone on his or her list. They are a doorway to people we would not have been able to meet. Just like when I do a PBR in a new recruit's home, I am not there only to sign up some new people and make a buck that night. I am there to recruit *through* them and book a next round of PBRs in their homes!

Don't see people just for who they are as individuals, but rather who they can also lead you to. Every dud knows a stud. So even if they are not very ambitious, everyone knows ambitious people. That is why we are "Networkers" … we *network* through people.

URGENCY AND FEAR OF LOSS

The most common reason most people do not succeed in building a large team or business is their *lack* of *urgency*. When you show the prospect that you have no urgency, they will have none either. First off, if you do not convey that there is something big going on with the growth of your company, you will not even attract your prospect's interest in the first place. So the first key is piquing their interest to look at a business that is on the front end of a trend. Let's assume you got their attention and they have seen your presentation … now how do you get them to sign up on the spot? This is important because every day that ticks by after the presentation and they have not joined, the odds of them doing so drop by around 10 percent per day. With dedicated follow-up for months and years, there is still a chance — but why create that scenario of cat and mouse when you can close them on the spot using urgency and fear of loss?

DANGLE THE CARROT

One way you can create urgency is to use something that is about to take place with the company as something they will not want to miss out on. This might be a new product launch, a new country opening, a new promotion, etc. But without such a stimulant, you can create your own sense of urgency by "dangling the carrot" in front of their face. You do this by letting your prospect know that you have several others you are meeting with over the next few days who will be joining the business … and if your prospect acts now and submits their application to join, you will put those next recruits under them. By getting those recruits placed under them, you explain how this would potentially create passive, override income in their pocket from people *you* are giving to them based on them joining first. People are motivated by the potential for gain, and even more so by the fear of loss of possible profits they would miss out on forever.

Here's how I do this:

"Jim, now you obviously see the value in our product and a huge opportunity in the business for yourself. On that alone, I bet you are ready to get started and begin building your business. But here's an even bigger kicker. I have several people I am talking with this week who are very interested in the business as well, and I expect to also bring them on board. Here's what is going to happen: By you getting your application submitted right now, before those people do, they are going to be placed onto *your* team. You beat them to the punch, and now you are able to earn override income on the business they bring to the company forever! In essence, I am already helping you get into profit mode that fast! So let's get your application done, and toast to what we are going to do together to both create an incredible income."

Your posture and confidence are everything. If you act like you are questioning whether they will join, they will pick up on that. Close with confidence. Of course they are joining! Who would choose to miss out on this?

SHOPPING THE APP

Another way to create urgency to close prospects is to use a recruit's application already in hand. Once you sign up that new recruit, before you put them into The System, leverage it! Call every prospect on your list and say this:

"Hey Beth, the business we talked about and you have been thinking of joining … well, I've got a big gift for you! I just signed up a really sharp person, James, and he is super excited about all the people he is making appointments to go meet with and sell to. I am getting ready to put James' application into the system, but I wanted to let you get in before him and I will place him *under* you on your team! This would mean I would let you earn override income on all the business he is going to bring in — forever! I figured you could use a break of good luck and I want to make your day. Are you by your computer so you can fill out your application, so I can put James under you today?"

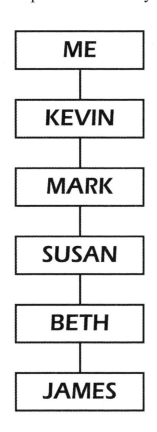

The great thing about "shopping James' app" is that you now got Beth's app. So now you have two apps to shop around to entice more and more prospects to finally get off the fence and join. I have done this often, and one time I recruited nine people in *one day* — all stemming from one recruit's app and shopping it over and over! I used James to get Beth. Then I used James and Beth to recruit Susan. Then I use all three to recruit Mark. And then I use all four to get Kevin, and so on. Then I put them straight down in a line, one under the other.

So in effect, recruiting James really helped me close several prospects! Again, people don't want to miss out on overrides from a team you can help them build — and that you are building *anyway*. Be sure to get really good at painting the picture and vision for what their team is going to look like a year from now, and how the income will flow. Get their head into the game, and their application will quickly follow.

GET IN VS. LET IN

Success in recruiting is a mindset and a philosophy. Many people are out there prospecting every day trying to *get* people into their business. This projects an air of need. On the other hand, I prospect people to see if I will *let* them into my business. This projects a posture of strength and confidence.

The difference is akin to *hunting* versus *fishing*. A hunter stalks his prey. He goes after his target. You know a hunter recruiter because they often say, "I got one!" Nobody likes to be "gotten." A fisherman does not go after fish. Rather, he selects what he feels is the bait/lure the fish might like ... then throws the bait out there and reels it in slowly attempting to attract the fish. Once a fish bites, he tries to hook the fish and gingerly draws it in without allowing the fish to jump off. Sometimes the drag is loosened so that if the fish swims away with the line, the tension will not be so much that it snaps the line. A good fisherman knows how to play with the fish while patiently reeling it in.

Do you notice a vast difference? Hunters may sometimes recruit someone, but that likely amounted to a hard sell. This does not duplicate very well. The fisherman just tosses the opportunity (lure/tool) out there, and waits for the fish to bite. If the fish are hungry, they will bite. I personally believe I have been a big recruiter because I *love* to fish. I love trying to figure out the right lure, the right way to retrieve my cast, the right tides to fish, and the best place to go. It's a game, a challenge. I do not get bummed out or discouraged if I cast my lure 30 times with no bites. I might go the whole day without a catch. That's OK. I enjoyed it, because it's what I love to do. That's how I feel about my network marketing business. It's a business and a hobby all rolled into one. Some people have work, and then they have a hobby they pursue in any free time they can find. I get to do both at the same time, all the time! And by the way, I like to have many lines in the water all at once.

A key difference between hunters and fishers of recruits is posture. Hunters convey a *need* to get that person into their business. The posture of fishers is more like they *might let* you into their business — *if* you are lucky. They are nonchalant and cool. They are patient and deliberate. So don't chase people like a hunter, but rather share your opportunity and offer your prospects a chance to interview for a spot on your team.

MASSIVE COMMUNICATION = MASSIVE INCOME

In 1998, my mentor said to me, "The size of your phone bill will determine the size of your check." So I decided that I would use my phone all day and night and run up my bill! I was hungry and ambitious, and I took him at his word. He was a millionaire in this industry, and I believed he was right. So I learned through my own experience that "Massive Communication = Massive Income." We are in the people business or the people-moving business. Thus, we are in the communication business. In order to move people to action, we must communicate with them. If I want to recruit people, I need to communicate my business opportunity to my prospects. If I want my downline to get their prospects on a conference call or to an event, I must promote this by communicating it to them. Remember this — we are *networkers*. We get paid to connect and communicate on a personal level. That is why the companies we are distributors for pay us so much money. A company cannot reach and connect with people on a personal level. It just isn't possible. That is the value we bring, and that we *must* bring, if we expect to earn income.

In recent years, so many networkers have been fooled into thinking/hoping that sending emails, texts, or social media messages would create the connection with people. While I admit that these can serve a purpose, they will never replace the *need* for human interaction. Did you miss it? The word I just used was *interaction*. This means you are not just sending out your ideas, thoughts, or wishes. Rather, you are conveying these in an interactive, engaging way. Massive Communication could be mistaken for one-way communication from you outward. So instead, I change my premise to the need for "Massive Connection." We must connect with people. Connect our prospects' *need* with their *solution*, which is our product or opportunity. Connect our team members' goals with the proven activity we want them to engage in to succeed. And connect with each member of our teams, showing we really care about their success.

So how do I spend my time? I spend 25 percent of my day in each of the four areas demonstrated in the following illustration:

TIME	
25%	**25%**
Contacting my own new prospects to recruit	Following up on my own existing prospects on my list
Doing three-way calls/third-party closes for my team	Calling my team to promote something and inspire action
25%	**25%**

This brings us back to *IPA* (Income Producing Activity). If you are not talking to a prospect (yours or your team's) to bring them to a decision, you are not making money. So 75 percent of my time is devoted to this, always. Even now, after earning more than $15 Million (and counting), I still honor this strategy. Why? Because what got me here will keep taking me up the elevator shaft. Twenty-five percent of my time is focused on leadership/management-type activity. I see so many networkers slow down on their prospecting and follow-ups, and focus more on motivating their team. They go from leading by example to telling people what to do. I prefer to *show them* what I do, and ask them if they can follow my lead. It has not failed me yet … but maybe that is because I am not lazy, and I care about my team members achieving *their goals*.

WELCOME CALLS

Immediately when you recruit a new person onto your team, you must get them on "Welcome Calls" with at least two or three of your upline. By introducing this new, often skeptical, person to people who are already successful in the business, you make the business more real to them. This reaffirms their good decision to join the company and increases their belief in the opportunity. The last thing you want your recruit to do is have their only association with the company be *you*. Forbid the idea that they do not see you as someone they aspire to be like. You want them to meet people they will be inspired by, and trust that their future is in the hands of good mentors. This will also make them feel like they are part of a team. Remember that people will be less likely to quit on a team than they will on themselves.

Here are the *six* items for the upline to address on this Welcome Call (5-7 minutes maximum):

1. Tell your story

2. Ask for their *why*

3. Paint the vision of the company, then for the recruit's future

4. Explain and book their PBR and PCC, tell a PBR success story

5. Encourage Game Plan Interview with sponsor or veteran upline

6. Promote training class and weekly briefing

7. Edify their sponsor, and the two full-time upline leaders they will be working with.

AM I A GREAT SPONSOR?

One of the common reasons I hear from people who quit their network marketing business is because they did not have a "good sponsor." So what does it mean to be a good sponsor? I believe it has much to do with being a great example of work ethic, discipline, integrity, belief, reliability, and vision. People want to follow someone who is a visionary — a leader who sees great things ahead and can lead the way to building something grand. A great sponsor believes in the vision, in himself, and in his people.

You will quickly kill off any team you build if they sense that your mission is to recruit some people and then sit back and wait for them to start making you money. Nobody wants to make money for his or her upline. Rather, they want their upline to earn the overrides that will be generated. Your team expects that you will work hard to help them succeed, and in return the comp plan will automatically reward you for doing the work. So a good sponsor puts the needs of his/ her people first, helps them make money first, and possesses a strong work ethic. He leads by positive example doing the activity that he wants his team to emulate. That is one of the main reasons why I built one of the largest teams in the entire industry in the decade 2000-2010 (more than 300,000 reps). I never let anyone feel like they were out-working me. I heard so many compliments over the years that they admired how hard I worked in such a focused way. Folks, that's what it takes! *Consistent* work ethic. Period.

Working is key, but so is doing it with belief, passion, and energy. A great sponsor *inspires* others to believe in their dreams and to go for it. You constantly have to be "on," meaning your music must be positive and uplifting. Never speak negatively or disbelieving to your downline — *ever*! Negative always goes upline; positive always goes everywhere (your upline needs to hear positive from you, too).

Discipline is something that people notice. They know whether you are making your calls, showing up to events, listening to team calls, reading good books, and staying in Phase One (personally prospecting). They also can see whether you are a disciplined leader they wish to follow by your health, fitness, diet, and finances. People will only want to follow someone they see as a good role model in all areas of life. So the more well-rounded your disciplines are, the better.

Integrity is a big one. Do what you say you are going to do. If you promise to give someone some tools, do it. If you say you will give them a recruit, do it. Do what is right and ethical. Never steal anything from anyone. Don't lie about your income. Do not have affairs with anyone in your business. *Integrity is doing what's right when nobody is looking.* Just remember, time will expose or promote everyone. Let your actions over time promote you as a truly amazing example of leadership and goodness.

Are you reliable? Have you ever promised a recruit you would do a call for them, but then you were not available when promised? Or a PBR? Did you tell a recruit you would make some calls to their list, but never got around to it? Have you offered up an incentive, but never honored it? When your recruits or team feel that they cannot count on you, then you are toast. They will never truly follow you, and will soon leave you. Be a man or woman of your word. Be accessible as much as you can be. Be a servant leader by putting their interests first. Trust me, your massive following of supporters will boost you up in glory in the end if you do.

LONG DISTANCE SPONSORING

I have had quite a few prospects tell me that they were interested in my business, but wanted to find themselves someone to sponsor them in their local marketplace instead. They insisted they would need in-person training and hand holding in order to succeed. So I had to share with them what my upline taught me.

My active upline, who became my main mentor in my beginning years, was in Texas, while I lived and built in Maryland. I told him I wished he lived in Maryland so he could help me more. He said to me, "No, you don't want that. If my presence with you is required to succeed, that would mean you will never be able to sponsor someone out-of-state and help them to succeed. Do you want your team to only be limited to your particular state, or to span all across the continent? Because if a local mentor was a requirement to succeed, you could never accomplish your goal. A local sponsor can only teach you how to build *locally*. I can teach you to succeed all the way from here in Texas, thereby showing you exactly how to duplicate that with all of the countless people you wish to sponsor and train all over the country."

Wow, this was an awakening! I have shared this premise with every long distance prospect, and it is rare that this message doesn't fix their thinking. Having a long distance mentor also gave me the space and breathing room to become a strong independent leader. Of course, I never broke away from my upline. We stayed interconnected. But I became a market leader. Sometimes having a great upline, especially locally, causes most people to never *need* to become great leaders … so they often don't.

When long distance sponsoring, not much changes,

really. You still promote and plug people into The System. The only thing that you cannot do is be there physically for PBRs, but you can call into them via speaker phone to close them out after the video. And you can't be there at briefings to circle up. But you will teach your upcoming leaders to step up and be the leader to take that role. For everything else, you are a phone call away just like you would be if you were only 10 miles down the road. Don't let long distance building be scary to you. With phones and technology today, the world is basically now your back yard. You can support your team and build community by leveraging The System. Whatever you expect happens. So expect to build across the map very quickly.

GRAB THEIR TOP TEN

From the moment you recruit someone, the race is on. *Those first seven days are critical!* You are trying to get them a sale or a recruit before they quit. Every day that ticks by without some success, their fire is dying down. The excitement they first had when they joined, and the feeling that they will go sign up the world, is declining. They are talking to people who are not interested. Self-doubt starts kicking in. They are wondering if they made a good decision, or if they even want to invest any more time into this pursuit.

So the race is on for you to help them work their contact list. They need to have their decision to get started reinforced by someone they know buying the product or becoming a part of their team. Of course, getting a recruit goes miles further in reinforcing their business decision, but any win will do. Remember that they don't know what to say when they are calling their prospects. They are worried about this. They may work through the fear and make some calls, but surely we cannot expect that those first calls will be brilliant. We want them to persevere making these calls anyway. If they are going to learn to swim, they've got to get into the pool and start flapping around.

As the great upline networker you are (or are becoming), you will not allow your success and theirs to be left in their hands alone. You are going to get a copy of their list and discuss who the top 10 sharpest, most ambitious contacts are on it. Then you will leverage your mutual connection and make these calls yourself. Your goal may be to sell the product, or to recruit them. Either way, the new recruit will let you call these 10 while they cut their teeth on the others on their list.

One thing that does help is having the recruit send a short text or email to these top 10 to warm it up for you first. So the day you are going to start calling, have them send a message something like:

"Hi John, a gentleman named _____ is going to call you today about something very important and private. Be sure to take his call for a few minutes. We'll talk later."

Now their prospects will be looking out for and willing to take your call.

This is not the only time you will hear the topic in this book, and for good reason. To build your downline, all you need to do is help your people recruit their contacts. Let them approach some, and you approach the cream of their crop. As you taproot down, doing this for each recruit who joins, you will watch your team grow level by level.

If you help each recruit get their first recruit within their first week, in one year you are 52 levels deep! And that's just what *you* did ... not including what their other legs will contribute! But if you don't help them recruit someone in their first week, you will likely have lost them and will have to keep recruiting their replacements *Speed* and *urgency* are everything! Get focused on every recruit who joins your team immediately (even those brought in way below you by others). Reach down, grab them, and run!

5

Motivate Your Empire

LEADERSHIP VS. MANAGEMENT

Years ago, all the talk was about how great management was the key to a company's success. These days the paradigm has shifted, and we see *leadership* as paramount to success. There is a *huge* difference between the two … and when you get it, you will get why some people make it big in network marketing and others do not.

Managers see it as their task to get others to do what the company wants them to do. Leaders get the people to *want* to do (themselves) whatever the company is wanting.

Can you clearly see the difference? If you work for a company and your manager wants you to go sell 10 units this month, that manager is going to "manage" you by convincing you why this goal must be met. Managers use tactics based on the "carrot or the stick." Sell 10 units or else you will not keep your job. So fear of losing your job is used to manipulate you into motivation. Or they might dangle a promotion in your face to get you to work harder. Management tactics do not work very well. Yet even if they achieve the intended result, the employee is not connected emotionally with the process and, therefore, the motivation cannot be lasting.

A leader, on the other hand, takes a completely different approach. Leaders "lead" people. They share a vision that embodies both the company *and* the person — *together*. They paint a picture that depicts the company winning only by the individual person winning as well. Leaders get "buy in" from the individual by tuning him/her into their own favorite radio station — WIIFM — *What's In It For Me*. A good leader can get people to *want* to hit their goals for their own reasons, not for the leader or for the company. Of course the goals ought to be congruent for all involved. But when you motivate a person by that which motivates him, you essentially connect the person's own desires to that of the company. Thus, he takes ownership of the task at hand, and will be far more self-motivated and need less prodding to do the job well.

Do you see how this applies to building a network marketing organization? If you try to *manage* your team, they will see that you are only looking out for your goals … what *you* want them to do, and how much money *you* want them to make you. I often see most networkers fall into management mode. They stop doing the recruiting and selling themselves, and turn to trying to be a dictator over their team by telling everyone what they ought to be doing. The team soon turns on this upline "manager," but usually not in a mutiny. What generally happens is they just fade away and drop out of the business. They did not join this industry to have a boss, and they certainly won't be inspired by one to stick around or produce.

Leaders in our industry are those who actually care about the dreams and desires of their team. Leaders guide, they don't dictate. They try to help their team members see the reasons to want to do certain activities; they don't expect them to do them. Leaders are good at selling their team on the *vision* of the company, the team, and the person. Leaders elicit others to rise up and perform at their optimal potential. How do leaders do this? They get into the head of each person, figure out what makes that person tick, and then align their rudder to guide the ship in the same direction as the team and the overall goals. That creates congruence between the team and all team members.

A good leader knows the *why* (reason the person is building this business) of each and every person he or she is leading. You must *focus on building people* instead of *getting sales*. A leader wants to create other leaders. Your goal should be to duplicate yourself. And the ultimate success is to have many people under you who out-earn you, and get more recognition than you. That is when you know you have succeeded here.

Here is a list of what leaders must do. Leaders must:

- Solve problems

- Turn challenges into positives

- Keep downline on track and plugged into The System

- Promote calls, events, promotions

- Run contests for the team

- Help people set goals

- Inspire/motivate using stories

- Teach how to's

- Read personal development books and promote the same

- Be a good financial example by being smart with their money

- Build team culture

- Never fracture from the upline or system

- Always edify — thus will get edified

- Allow themselves to be led — even Michael Jordan had a coach

- Be responsible

- Be accessible

- Be reliable

- Be empowering

- Be caring

- Track their business — know their numbers

- Help track downline's business/goals

- Not want to remain a follower

- Be in pursuit of mastery

- Become a better speaker — calls, PBRs, PCCs, briefings, trainings

- Recognize others for accomplishments

- Give away credit, accept blame

- Not get content/complacent

- Raise the lid for their team

- Sit in the front row at events, not stand in the back being cool

- Help make things happen

- Communicate massively

- Connect massively

Remember that life is going to tear your people's focus away from their business. Life happens, and we can't stop that. But as a leader you must know this, and constantly "distract your team from their distractions." In other words, if someone is going through a divorce, a leader will help him or her to focus on the positives of their business instead of dwelling on the loss in their life. Think of all the distractions people have — football, TV shows, kids' activities, illness, relationship troubles, family commitments, vacations, bad weather, lack of money, jobs, car issues, etc. We cannot stop these things from being true. But we can keep bringing their attention back onto their network marketing business. By focusing them on doing the activities required to win here, they will eventually succeed. And as you can imagine, success brings a certain ease. More money and more time freedom will make some problems go away, and make others easier to handle. And living life with more passion will stem from them existing in this personal development environment we are entrenched in.

HOW TO PAINT THE VISION

"Where there is no vision, the people perish." We've all heard this, but most do not understand how to live by it. Few people in the world have ever sat down for even an hour to design their life. They have no connection to a vision that drives them. They do not wake up with a sense of purpose each morning, raring to go conquer the world and summit the mountain. Monotony and a feeling of being unfulfilled often strain their lives. This is because they lack a vision. Creating a vision should be taught in school, but it is not. Parents with no vision certainly cannot teach it to their children. Helen Keller was asked decades ago what could be worse than being blind. Her response was, "The only thing worse than being blind is having sight but no vision."

First, you must have a personal vision before you can paint one for your team members. So let me paint the vision of your future for you (and you copy this with your team).

Let's look out several years from now.

Your life took an amazing turn for the best when you started your new network marketing business. That decision coupled with solid work ethic put you in this place you are now. Monetarily, you have more than you can spend. Just the interest and dividends coming passively from your investments are more than you ever made working full-time in your past. Your income flows from the efforts of others now, and from a huge customer base that you built up over the years. You never look at the price when reading the menus while dining out. You take an exotic vacation every three months to some place new and exciting. You walk new beaches around the world on week-days when others are stuck in office buildings back home.

Speaking of your home — you have three of them, each in different locales and decked with lavish décor that you spent time laboring over with care. Your family enjoys time in the different homes, and each feels so very homey. You have true time freedom, and you set your own schedule to satisfy your every whim. You take missions trips. You give of your time to charitable causes that make your heart beat and bring tears to your eyes. You give to your church more money than you ever made in a year from your job.

You have put in place a legacy that will survive you, that will be enjoyed and empower many generations after you. The respect and admiration you receive from your family and friends make you feel so proud, yet humble.

All of the worldly things have had an inverse effect on you. The trappings of your success were pride invoking along the way, but now that you are on the other side of money and success ... you give the credit upward and understand to Whom you belong.

How is that for a vision of your future? Does it excite you to know this is waiting for you? Do you think this would inspire a maniac work ethic in those for whom you paint such a picture of their future? The biggest leaders in our industry have become very good at painting pictures of a future vision for others. Get good at this. Once you have the vision painted in your head, make it visual too. Create a "Dream Board" or a "Vision Board." I took a 2 ½ x 3 ½-foot board and glued pictures of my future on it when I began my network marketing journey in this company. I had pictures of a happy family with kids on a beach, a beautiful home, beach front property in Turks and Caicos, exotic sports cars, a yacht, a speaker on a big stage, etc.

What's amazing is that I now have just about everything on that board except for a yacht. What is interesting is that my new dream board now has things like the Sunshine Kids charity for kids with cancer, friends, family, and the goal of helping 100 more people on my team to reach the Millionaire Club. It does show evidence that once you get to where you want to go, your priorities can change and other things become bigger drivers for you. It's OK if your goals right now are all about you. If you are honest about what drives you, let it drive you. Later on you can add to your vision and include things that may not be directed towards yourself.

I do believe that trying to help others and putti
eryone else first keeps most people from ever getting ....-
selves into a position to truly have a more magnificent impact.
For example, I felt that if I gave less of my time and money
earlier on in life, and focused my attention on achievement,
this would allow me far greater resources to have more impact in the future. In my mind, I feel this is absolutely what
has happened. I would rather put off giving $1,000 to charity
when it was hard to afford and invest it, so that later I could
give $100,000. Instead of spending five hours a week of my
time with one charity, what if I use that time to create a massive team of thousands of people who can now afford to each
spend five hours of their week doing so? So my five hours
being diverted ends up resulting in 5,000 hours of time spent
blessing others. We can delay personal gratification, as well
as selflessness. I am not here to dictate what you do with your
success. My aim in this book is to get you to the top of the
mountain, and holding onto hope that you remain grounded
and give back along the way. The world needs more empowered, good leaders who care about others around them.

PRAISE PROGRESS

Recognition — babies cry for it, and men die for it. Of
course, most people start a business like this to pursue making money from it. But in any network marketing business,
the income they make early on will not be enough. There will
always be times when every distributor feels they need to
make more, faster. They may often get frustrated that success
isn't coming fast enough. So how do you keep them excited
about their business when their income is not pouring in yet?

The key is they have to feel that they are progressing towards their goals. If they feel like their business is moving forward and growing, they will stay after it. If they feel like they are stuck, they may give up. But this business is more than just about the money. It is about success, winning, and appreciation. It is about feeling a sense of contribution, and being part of a team.

People will do more of what they get recognized for. So if you want your distributors to make more sales, applaud them when they make one. Make a big deal about it. After all, it may have been quite hard for them to finally sign up that recruit or make that elusive sale. That one victory may not have netted them much money in and of itself … but it is still a victory. When they get a phone call to congratulate them, or they hear their name mentioned on a conference call or at a meeting, they will glow on the inside. It'll put a bounce in their step. They will feel successful. And because they love feeling this way, they will want to do it over and over so that they can be made to feel this way again. And off they will go to get another sale! And this time, they will want to top the last victory by making two sales to receive another accolade. And once they achieve this next win and receive the adoration and spotlight, they will speed off to get three or four more to redeem this for even more applause. I am telling you that if you praise every small win, you will inspire your team members to keep winning.

Not only do you want to praise the success, you also want to praise progress. Maybe you have a new recruit who holds a PBR in their home in their first week, but no prospects show up. Praise them for doing the activity and trying! They cannot control the results, but they did their best and should feel great about it. If you show them your respect for their effort, they will be encouraged enough to stay in the game and give it another shot. As long as your downline members stay in the game, you will have chances to help them learn and improve. People will stay if they *feel good* and appreciated, even if they are not making the money they desire yet.

Ways to recognize your team members:

- Send out team emails and include shout outs

- Mention in team newsletters

- Show their name on team website and via social media

- Spotlight them on team training calls

- Send them gifts (personal development book with personal note inside)

- Give them dinner for two, or movie tickets

- Invite them onto stage at events to tell their story

- Reward them by giving them a recruit

CONTESTS TO CREATE ACTIVITY

Over the years, I have always tried to be creative and come up with contests or promotions that would drive behavior. People like to be challenged, and the ambitious ones o the occasion. I try to think of ideas that everyone can participate in. I base some of them on activity alone, and some are based on results.

Activity-Based Contests:

- Get "100 No's" in a month Challenge (get prospects to listen to a sizzle call) — We give everyone a sheet with 100 *No's* on the page, and five *Yes*es. Each person is to make exposures and mark off the responses they get, seeing if they can get five people to say *Yes* to look at the business before 100 people say *No*.

- PBR Contest — who can have the biggest guest attendance at their in-home PBR presentation?

- PCC Contest — who can get the most prospects on their Private Conference Call?

- Briefing Contest — who can get the most guests to show up to the weekly business briefing?

Results-Based Contests:

- Top Recruiter of the Month/Top 20 Recruiters

- Top Sales Producer

- Upline who helps the most Rank Advancements in their downline for the month

The company comp plan should already have plenty of

financial reward for the results. So as an upline leader, when you can reward activity and give recognition for every little or big victory — you will lead an army of people to success.

INCLUSION/EXCLUSION

One of the greatest motivators for us all is our deep desire to be *included*. As a kid, how did you feel about getting picked for a sports team? Or being invited, or not invited, to a birthday party? Everyone wants to be a part of the "in crowd," and we all want to feel important.

What my upline and mentors did to me early on is made me want to earn their respect and my chances to join their inner circle. I wanted to be on the inside. Because I understood that our associations work hard on us, I wanted to associate with the winners. If there was a contest to win a spot at a leaders' dinner, I won it. If there was a special trip with the top producers, I won it. Being included meant the world to me. And believe it or not, it means that much to most people.

As a leader of your team, your job is to come up with ways to create this environment. Think up activities that only the producers and team builders can participate in. Make it exciting, and encourage everyone to strongly desire his or her way in. Special dinners, weekend trips, special seating at events, reserved parking, special name badges, special recognition page on the team website ... and be sure to use social media and communication avenues to publicize it often.

Your goal is to make this something for people to strive for, and have pride in being included. Just keep in mind you do not want to go too far, to the point that you make everyone else feel like they are not valued or worthy just because they haven't earned the inclusion — *yet*. The fact is, by them just being on the team and in the business is its own inclusion factor. The masses out there have not even been let into the arena yet.

CREATE TEAM CULTURE

You have heard that "Teamwork Makes the Dream Work." This is repeated often because it carries much truth. The whole reason you are in network marketing is because you don't want to be a salesperson constantly doing all of the selling. That would be yet another *job*. Your end game here is to have a large team of people each making a few sales a month/week, which will generate passive cash flow into your bank account — without you having to do the selling. This "team" thing goes well beyond who is making the sales. At first glance, most everyone sees this and wants a team to go sell and make them money. But it isn't that easy. It takes a good recruiter to bring people into the business. But it takes a great leader to assemble these people into working together as a team. They can sell by themselves, but that might get old and they might quit. Teams keep people engaged and in the game.

I have watched many people go out and recruit a whole ton of individuals into their downline. But they remained individuals, each independently attempting to build their own businesses. Think about that. Yes, as a networker you are in business *for* yourself, but should not be by yourself. It gets very lonely if you are not on a team. Who will you share your victories with? Who will lift you up when you feel down and maybe keep you from giving up? I would venture to say that

90 percent of people who quit their network marketing business do so because they felt they did not have the support they needed to learn how to succeed. I know this because I have heard it thousands of times from those who have quit. We say that people should not blame their sponsor for their lack of success. But in reality, unless someone upline pulls people together and creates a winning team environment, people will always come in and quit rather quickly. The recruits are buying not only into a company and business, but they also need to be part of a team and family that cares about them personally.

People want to be part of something bigger than themselves. People will often work harder to help the team achieve its goal than they will for their own goals. This assumes the team makes them feel important as an integral part, and that it cares about them. I have seen distributors who did nothing all month long to build their own business or make money for themselves ... but when the team they were a part of needed a few more sales to hit a team goal, that person went out and hustled up a few sales they otherwise would not have created for themselves. Why is this? Well, to some people the money is not their biggest driving force. Rather, they want to feel important, respected, and know that they matter. They want to make a difference and be loved. Do you realize that if you are only talking to your downline distributors about making money, you are missing the things that are more motivating to them than just making money?

Love, respect, purpose, importance, and feeling like they can make a difference are some of the key human drivers. Commissions are important, but not enough to compel people to act consistently. Quite frankly, why do people want to make huge amounts of money? If you think about it, you will conclude that maybe it is because if they are wealthy others might respect them more. Or they could afford to do nice things for people (which garners appreciation). Or they will feel more important or in control.

So how does all of this play into "creating team culture?" As a leader who wants to build something huge and significant, you will want to create an environment that is conducive to achieving these drivers. Here are some ideas that can be part of creating this:

1. **Purpose** — Everyone wants to feel excited knowing that his or her efforts are serving a greater good. So your team should create a Mission Statement that lays out what this "greater good" is.

2. **Belonging** — Yes, the distributor is part of the overall networking industry, and even a part of their particular company. But just like in football, being in the NFL is great, but a player needs to be passionate about playing for a particular team. There needs to be a sense of pride/ownership.

3. **Inspiration** — When a team is in place, inspiration will not always have to come from the leader at the very top. Every success story that happens for any individual within the team will inspire the others if showcased properly and immediately.

4. **Accountability** — When in business for yourself and left by yourself, it is easy to hide in the shadows and not put forth effort. This happens very

often, and is why many people end up quitting. But if the team leader is pulling people together, publicly coordinating activities, and then discussing the outcomes as a team, there is less chance of the shadows taking away your distributors.

5. **Recognition** — You can create team contests or challenges for doing certain activities, or for getting certain results, and then publicly recognize them for it. Recognition is more motivating than money. Men die for it, and babies cry for it. You can never recognize people enough. Recognize what you want them to do more of.

6. **Support** — Your people will need emotional support along the way as they encounter disappointments. When they are having a bad day, the team can reach out and lift their spirits/resell them on their *why* and dream. When a person has a great day, they can share the story with the team. This will fire the rest up to go out and grab success as well.

To create this team culture, here are some things you can do:

1. **Weekly Team Conference Calls** — This is a chance to not only train, but also to recognize and to allow others to speak and be developed into leaders.

2. **Team Website** — Here you can aggregate all sorts of support information and material, as well as recognition.

3. **Team Events** — Getting together for training, recognition, and to rally the energy and spirit. This is where the relationships that are so vital to team culture can be best created and nurtured.

4. **Fun Activities** — You don't want to be all business and no play ... so get the team together and let your hair down, too! Bowling, fishing, cookouts, camping trips ... anything where you do things together.

5. **Charity/Philanthropy** — Pull your team together and decide on one or two causes they feel strongly about supporting. Then organize everyone to donate their time together to these activities.

Just make sure that people know, *when the team wins ... everyone wins.* Everyone will not be the starting quarterback or the MVP of the game. They may not have even contributed a single sale. But they tried, and their energy and spirit were vital to the team's success. Never forget this. Never forget that Michael Jordan was cut from his high school basketball team. If you make *everyone* feel special, important, and respected, you might just be surprised that some might suddenly become your top producers. A caring team leader will instill his/her values into the team culture.

CALL PARTIES

Promoting events is one of the most important skills or activities we must engage in. If we get prospects to briefings, we will recruit them. If we get our downline to events, they will get trained and inspired. Every networker spends time sitting on the phone making calls to prospects and team members. Sometimes it can get monotonous making calls day after day by ourselves. So we hold Call Parties to promote for each event.

Let's say, for example, we have a big business briefing on Saturday at 10 a.m. We select one person's house where a group of teammates can gather and bring their lists of prospects with them on Wednesday evening. Everyone spreads out and dials for dollars. Once we have a prospect on the phone and we share with them about the event to invite them, we edify someone in the house who is free and we pass the phone to them. That third-party person shares their short story and excitement about the business and confirms the invite for the briefing. Now the prospect has committed to two people — their friend *and* a stranger. They are much more likely to show up now.

We also have contests at call parties to see who gets the most guests confirmed for the event. The energy is in the air, and everyone has a great time making the dials. And when someone encounters a rude prospect, they hang up and everyone makes fun of the prospect for missing the opportunity that could have changed their life. Hey, there's nothing wrong with inserting a little fun into the equation!

These call parties also work great for uplines getting together to promote to their downlines to attend training events. Everyone comes over with their downline lists, and dials away. Something unique can be done here as well. We often have everyone swap downline lists. This way your downline is hearing from a fresh voice about why they should attend the event, rather than hearing from the same old *you*! A prophet is never heard in his own backyard, to modify an old saying. In other words, after a while, your team doesn't snap into gear very fast anymore when you are always the one asking them to do something. But when someone else calls, they tend to hear the same message in a different way. So calling each other's downlines works wonders.

SUCCESS COMPRESSION

It is easier to build this business fast than slow. Instead of talking to 10 people in a week, it is more powerful to call all 10 in one day. Emotion and energy rises when you have lots of action going on all at once. When I started with the company that I made more than $15 Million in (as of this writing), *I made a list of 200 people. I called every last one of them in my first three days.* Everyone I knew got a call. I was blowing by and going Mach II with my hair on fire! Light yourself on fire, and people will come from miles around to watch you burn! People were most likely drawn to my excitement more than anything. They figured I must be onto something big to be calling them with such *urgency*.

I was brief. I *said less* to *more people*. My goal was to contact and invite, and get off the phone. I was just promoting events and filling seats. I compressed time frames. Here's what some people do relative to what I did.

Some make 200 phone calls in three *years*.
Some make 200 phone calls in three *months*.
Some make 200 phone calls in three *weeks*.
Some make 200 phone calls in three *days*.

Which route will create the most excitement and explosive result?

Take a barrel of gunpowder and …

Spread it out over a state
Spread it out over a town
Spread it out over a mile
Spread it out over an acre
Spread it out over a sandbox

Then throw a lit match. Which will cause an explosion? Exactly … the powder that is compressed into the smallest area!

Explosive blitzes are used to create this kind of explosion in your business. A blitz is when you get a group of people on your team to come together to focus on tripling their efforts on a particular activity. For example, we do "Tool Blitzes." We have cases of magazines or DVDs or books and everyone meets in a parking lot. They each get dozens of tools and put their contact info labels on them. Then everyone goes out for two to three hours in pairs and canvasses the local area exposing people to information about our company. They go into car dealerships, stores, parks, sidewalks … basically anywhere they can meet people. At the end of the blitz period, everyone returns back to the meeting place and compares notes. We often give prizes to those who got the most phone numbers, and everyone else chips in to buy the winner lunch or dinner.

I love tool blitzes because whoever gets the most tools into the marketplace will make the most money. This is not

g ... it's a fact. I proved it! My team has moved
ɔols into the hands of people across the country.
ᴛᴏᴏʟs ᴜo ᴛнe presentations for us ... all we have to do is get
people to review them.

THE 90-DAY RUN

You really *can* change your life in 90 days. I am living proof. One of my mentors told me that if I create a great
income success story in my first 90 days, I would be able to
create so much momentum that it could potentially carry me
for the rest of my career. So I took him at his word and ran
very hard. "Ninety days of pain for a lifetime of gain!" So
true, let me tell you! I was willing to pay the short-term price
for long-term success.

Part of the power in doing this run in your *first* 90 days
of your business lies in the fact that you are creating a compelling story. For the rest of your career, you will be able to
answer every prospect's question of "How much money did
you make when you first joined" with an exciting response
that will motivate them. If you don't get off to a good start
and do much, that story will not exactly be compelling in your
recruiting pitch, will it? But if you made an extra $2,000+ in
the first couple of months, doing it only part-time ... now *that*
will turn some heads!

So my first 90 days was explosive. I gave it all I had,
and made many sacrifices. My income story was strong
(much more than that $2,000 mark), and I could already point
to success stories on my team. For the last 14 years, I have
repeated that story as a part of my pitch. But what I did was
not ride on the momentum created by just this first 90-day

run. I strung several of these runs together. I find that it is easy to create a plan and focus for 90 days like a laser. You can do this, believe me. Just work your plan hard, with a burning white-hot fire for three months .. then rest a minute. Then create the next run and do it one more time. I did these back-to-back sprints with the runners on my team. I found out it is way easier to build this business *fast* than it is to build it slow. Fast is like you are riding in a race car, while slow is like trying to push a car with its emergency brake on up a hill! Momentum is your best friend, and *big mo* is only found when you explode with activity in a condensed time frame.

You might look at the amount of frenzied effort we are talking about as if it's the *Insanity* workout that you might have seen on TV. The commercial shows people losing weight and getting in crazy shape in literally 30 days by virtually going non-stop through rigorous movements in the gym in condensed intervals. It makes my heart race just watching the ad! But focused, condensed efforts work. I like that insanity style. Give your business all you've got for a short window of time. If you have 10 hours a day, or if you only have two hours a day you devote to it, squeeze every last phone call and appointment you can muster from your body.

What does a 90-Day Game Plan look like?

Pull out your calendar. Select the 90-day window with a key focus on the end date. You want to have a distinct finish line with a huge event that you and your team are building towards. All of your efforts and recruiting will crescendo at this grand finale gala event! Everything you do with your team will be pointing towards this finish line. Establish a goal as a team for how many people will be in attendance. *Make it big!* Also project how many people will be at certain recognition and income levels by then. Every conversation with your team members will be about what their personal goals are for their 90-day run, and tracking their progress daily towards it.

Everyone needs to be on the same page. As far as devising the roadmap in everyone's calendars, start by laying in the big blocks first. So block out the times for your weekly briefings, your training classes, monthly training events, team conference calls, etc. This is The System infrastructure. Once this is in ink, then everyone works day and night to fill in every single blank space on the pages of their calendars. The more appointments for PBRs, PCCs, sit downs, webinars, tool blitzes and call sessions, the better. *Fill* 'em up! Ninety days of no spare time, no TV, no bowling, no travels … just focus!

Each week during this run, there will be accountability calls with each leg of your organization by each leader. Everyone reports their activities and results, and restates their goals and their commitment to achievement. Those who are on fire will be invited to share their stories of how they have succeeded so far. As a leader, be sure to "inspect what you expect." Overwhelming encouragement will be needed, because fatigue can set in for the less ambitious types, and for those who might be feeling like they are not getting their desired results yet. Your job is to keep yourself *and* your team on fire for this run. It will be your life for the next 90 days.

The Grand Finale finish line event needs to be exciting and magnificent. High-energy music, beautiful staging, and tons of recognition. Find something to recognize just about everyone for. Nobody fails. Some just succeed more than others. But this is a celebration of teamwork and effort, so spread the love to all.

INSPECT WHAT YOU EXPECT

You want your team to be doing PBRs with every new recruit they bring in. If they would do this every time, your business would take off and you would be well into the six-figures-a-year zone! So you teach it, preach it, scream it from the stage and repeat it on every conference call. You expect that they are getting the PBRs done. But it doesn't work that easy. You have to roll up your sleeves and go *inspect* what is happening. Get into the trenches and see exactly how your field leaders are getting their recruits started. See if they are doing a Game Plan Interview to establish the recruit's goals, making their list, booking a PBR and PCC date, and contacting and inviting. Only someone who wants to leave their financial future in their downline's hands would trust that everything is being done in plan.

You do not want to micromanage or be overbearing like a boss, but rather be their coach. In a caring way, ask to work alongside them through the process with a few of their next recruits to ensure The System is working properly for them. A good follower of The System will be excited to have their upline mentor there to assist them in their pursuit of mastery. Just be careful not to be too critical, and always praise progress. Even if they are messing it up, encourage them by recognizing them for their efforts. Then offer some course-correcting ideas to help them achieve better results. Tell stories of others who were doing that activity the same way, and how they did these few things differently and are now enjoying great success. Using stories always gets your point across in a way that resonates and sticks with them.

Your team will receive you well when they know you

have their best interest at heart in everything that you say and do. This trust is not given to you by title, but rather, you must earn it over time by them watching you serve them and others. Always be a servant leader, and you will win their hearts. When their hearts are with you, they will follow you and listen to your coaching.

6

The Mental Game

ACT AS IF

I think one of the things that helped me finally get traction in my business is when I started to *act* as *if* I was already one of the top money earners in the company. I began to carry myself with confidence. I walked into the room with my shoulders broad and chest puffed out. I was proud of who I was, or was becoming. I saw myself as a top team builder and coach. My affirmations were taking root. People started to see me as I saw myself. It was so cool to see. I wasn't faking it 'til I made it. I truly felt this way, like I was a star. Prospects began to listen to me. My team started to follow me.

Look, nobody wants to follow a dud. If you are not confident, why would you expect anyone to respect you or follow you? How can anyone be sold on you, if you aren't sold on yourself? What I did was project the confidence and belief I had in my awesome company, product, comp plan and mentors *onto myself*. They were all a part of what I represented. That was me, and I wore it well!

Act as if ... you are the top recruiter
Act as if ... you are a respected leader

Act as if … you have a huge team you are leading
Act as if … you are creating wealth
Act as if … you have helped many to succeed

Now the trick is to do this and act this way *with* humility, sincerity, and a servant's heart. This is tricky, and hard to do. Constantly check yourself. Be confident, but not cocky.

DON'T DRAG YOUR PAST FORWARD

How is *your* thought process and mindset affecting your recruits? In other words, what are you projecting onto them? The upline's past can quite often affect the present. Let's say the last 10 people you recruited did nothing and quit. They wouldn't even do a PBR in their home to get launched. Maybe they did nothing in the business and quit. Now you have these failures in the back of your mind when you are out trying to attract new recruits. Your own belief that they can succeed is diminished. But let's assume you are successful in recruiting your next person. It is likely that they will perform in the same fashion. *Why*? Because what you project onto your recruits is what they will do. If your belief has been shaken by the failures of your past recruits, you will unconsciously transfer your lack of belief into your new recruits. Your recruit will sense your doubt that they will make it happen — so guess what? — they won't. You will see the self-fulfillment of your own prophecy. Positive expectancy is crucial. You must expect each and every recruit to win. I know it may be hard to be positive when the last 10 recruits were duds but it is imperative that you wipe your mindset clean of the past misses and focus on the shot you are in the midst of taking. Every day is a new day. Every game is a new game. Every recruit is a new recruit.

How do you feel when your spouse, parent, or upline expresses their sincere belief in you? Doesn't that make you feel empowered and unstoppable? Of course it does. When your recruits are new, they need to borrow from your belief in them because they mostly don't believe in themselves yet. As uplines, we must *empower* our recruits. If they sense even in the least bit that we don't believe they will be successful, they will prove us right. I have seen this work in both directions. Empowering upline leaders develop amazing leaders under them through projection of strong belief in their people … while weak upline leadership kills every recruit who comes on board.

As an upline, what you *believe* matters. If you believe in PBRs, you will be five times more successful in getting your recruits to do them. If you are not seeing PBRs happening within your team, the buck stops at you. You are the leader, and what you believe, do, and teach, perpetuates. As sponsors, we have to constantly read personal development books on belief, attitude, leadership, and motivation. Our teams will thrive when we convey this to them. We need to be cognizant of how we are coming across to our teams. Just remember this … "If I believe in them, they will believe in themselves and in me."

What do I do with my recruits starting with Day One? Here's my plan:

Day 1 — Upon filling out their application, I do a few welcome calls with other team members. I do a short Game Plan Interview to establish their *why*, start making their list, and send them to the Getting Started page on my team website (here they learn about PBRs and PCCs). I also schedule them to get to a local briefing and training class.

Day 2 — Follow up to schedule their PBR and PCC (to happen within the first 3-5 days). I always have a good story to share with them about the product and a business success story.

Day 3 — Call to check in, keep them excited about the business, and keep them moving in the process.

Day 4/5 — Inspection call to check on progress. Share another story. Map out what it will take to promote them to the next level in the comp plan. (PBR and PCC should have taken place.)

From this point on, I continue to call them to keep them focused on the business. I know I have to distract them from the distractions in their lives. I keep sharing stories. I promote their next local event, the next team conference call, etc. I remain in constant communication with them, otherwise they feel orphaned and will quit. Massive Communication = Massive Income. My goal is to create a new friendship in conjunction with the business relationship.

As a good sponsor, I also give them Jim Rohn's "Building Your Network Marketing Business" CD and the Darren Hardy "Making the Shift" CD (find these on the Resources tab at www.FosterMentor.com). Your company most likely has a CD training program that comes in your kit, geared towards your specific business. I want them putting good information into their heads every day, so I ask them to turn off the radio and create their "Drive-Time University." These tools will create the proper mindset and philosophies in them daily, when I cannot be there to teach them personally. So I get tools doing some teaching for me.

The question I ask myself daily is: "Would I want to be sponsored by *me*?" My answer is always yes. I am proud to say that I impress myself with my caring and constant efforts to be the ultimate sponsor. If I could have me as my sponsor, I feel like I would already be making a million a month. What's awesome to think about is how great the network marketing profession would soar if more people became great sponsors breeding even more success.

STOP SELLING, START SOLVING

Nobody likes to be sold anything. Do you? People like to buy, but not be sold. So it only makes sense that as network marketers, we stop trying to sell prospects on our product or business, but rather help them to recognize problems in their life that our product or opportunity can solve. This goes with the saying, "Those who solve the biggest problems cash the biggest paychecks."

For example, if you are selling a nutritional product, don't focus on all the ingredients. Focus on any health/energy/weight challenges the prospect has (and wants to fix) and show how this product has helped others fix the very same problem. Or maybe you have a service that makes life easier. Focus less on the service offering and more on the direct benefits to eliminating stress in the prospect's life. Or maybe your product saves them money on something they already pay for. Don't just focus on the monetary savings, but go further and ask what they would do with the newfound $50 a month.

When you remember that we have one mouth and two ears, focus on listening twice as much as you do talking. Ask your prospect questions that will lead them to discuss problems they face. Once they open up and share, you must resist the temptation to immediately jump all over them with your sales pitch. Keep throwing it back to them by asking them more about the problem, and what ways they have tried to solve it. Ask them how important it is for them to find a solution. They will sell themselves on the need for what you want them to buy — and then you can *let them buy it.*

Customers who *buy* will stay your customers longer. They will be more likely to find reasons to like what they bought, versus finding remorse for what they were *sold*. Happy customers are also likely to give you referrals. Follow up with every customer and ensure that they are happy. People don't care how much you know until they know how much you care. When you are in the trust zone with them, they will feel comfortable referring people to you. And often they will convert from just being a customer to being a distributor.

OVERCOMING THE BOMBSHELLS (QUITTERS, NO-SHOWS, COMPANY CHANGES)

One of the few guarantees that I can make to you is that you will encounter many challenges along your journey to the top in this business. Prospects will stand you up at meetings. This is something you just have to get used to. Players on your team will quit after you have poured months or years of time and energy into them. This is much, much harder to handle. The company may even make directional changes or decisions that impact your business. This might make you feel like you are not in control. Your upline might leave for a new career path or business, leaving you feeling like an orphan.

I can honestly say that I have endured all of the above, and many times over. Was each incident fun? Of course not. Did I enjoy dealing with each occurrence as I was in the thick of it? Not really. Am I glad they happened? Well, if I could keep them from happening, I would have avoided them. But that's life … we cannot choose the problems that life (or our business) will throw at us. We *can* decide how we will respond to each challenge, and decide to grow from each experience. We shouldn't wish for things to be easier, rather we should wish to be better at dealing with them. In the face of each problem, I had to make the human decision of "Fight or Flight." Because my *why* was so strong, I chose *fight* each time. I was not going to shrink and run away. That would only ensure defeat and failure, and me staying the smaller person. By fighting through it, growing through it, I knew that I would become bigger and I would stay on course to achieve success.

Half of my leaders quit along the way, and I had to go recruit afresh and build new ones. There were times that my business hit plateaus and even declined, so I had to double up my efforts to regain momentum. My company made changes for the good of the distributors, but that still required adjustments every time. People who had left my company decided to turn and attack our credibility to try and sway others to follow them to other businesses. I had to take the high road defame their character, and let what's right happen in due course.

Believe me, I have been through it all. And to this very day, I am proud that I had the resolve and stick-to-it backbone to ride it out. I became better, and I feel that is why I have earned more than $15 Million. If I had tucked my tail and ran as I encountered any one of these challenges, I would be like the masses that do not achieve the big success they dream about. So my advice to every builder is this: Pick your business, stay on the path, grow through each and every obstacle or crisis, and come out the other side closer to your ultimate success. The only way to fail is to quit or let others knock you off course. Be strong, be brave, and be persistent.

YOUR MIND WILL PLAY TRICKS ON YOU

There are many days you will feel like you are riding a roller coaster. Just remember — *this* is *normal*. There is no way around it. You will have mental ups and downs in this journey of building your business. You get started in the business, and you are fired up! You have huge dreams and expectations. Then you get your first *no*, and your dream gets shattered. You stay with it, and go through some more rejection and finally recruit a great partner … woohoo! You are back on top of the world. Then that recruit quits the next week … you are back in the dumps. But then you recruit someone else, and you see hope again! And maybe your business starts to get traction and grows. But after a while, 90 percent of your downline has disappeared, and your mind plays tricks on you. Now you wonder if it is even worth recruiting anyone else, if most are only going to quit anyway. So now the phone weighs 300 pounds, and you just can't get motivated to make calls.

If this is going to happen regardless of who you are, and how good you are, what should you do? Immediately call your upline for some inspiration. Do not delay — make this call fast! Let the doctor kill the infection.

Here's what else I do. I remind myself daily that there are countless millionaires living their dream lives because they built their network marketing business and didn't quit. They made the calls and worked their way up from when they were down. So I did the same. I kept the dream in front of me every day. Any time I encountered a "Belief Shaker" — when something happened that shook my belief — I immediately reminded myself that those things happen all the time to every networker and every top earner. I am always working on my own belief to keep it strong, just like we have to work out our muscles to keep them strong. I feed my brain success stories constantly. We have to, especially because we hear so many negative stories and see so many people quit. I do not let losers and quitters suck me into their camp. I remain a warrior. Soldiers quit when they get injured … warriors quit when they've won. I don't dwell on the 50 calls I made yesterday without recruiting anyone. I just know that I am one recruit away from another financial explosion in my business. That next recruit might be my next stud who wants to run with me. Or maybe it will be my seventh one from now. All I know is that the studs will show up if I talk to enough people. History has proven this. I have no doubt about it.

I wish I could tell you that I had some magic "belief

shot" that I could inject you with, and you would never experience doubt in your business. Just remember, those who solve the biggest problems will cash the biggest paychecks. This means if you can handle all of the challenges that your business will throw at you, and if you can turn around and help your team to effectively handle the same, you will be wildly successful. How could you teach your team to get through the fires if you haven't gone through them yourself? So the goal is for you to stay the course, and keep your team on course with you. This *mental game* is 90 percent of the key to success in network marketing. People often question our industry or business model, pointing out the ratio of people who fail. Their ignorant assessment stems from them not knowing how to evaluate the business model in the first place. They think that 90 percent of people fail because the business is designed that way, where in fact, the network marketing model is designed for everyone to win. But only 10-20 percent actually stay the course and see it through to success. Do people attack the real estate brokerage business? Of course they don't. Yet 90 percent of people who get a real estate license never sell one house! Should brokers not keep recruiting more agents? Why doesn't the public get outraged over *that* business model? The broker makes overrides on all the agents they recruit on their sales. But those agents are also constantly churning and quitting.

One more very important thing! Don't bring forth your past failures and project them onto your next recruits. If the last five recruits did nothing or quit, you are likely to unconsciously convey your lack of belief that your new recruit will succeed. That's not only unfair to them, it also guarantees that you will kill your chances of winning.

STORIES INSPIRE

By now I hope you have heard many times that "Facts Tell, Stories Sell."

This is so true. Facts do not spark emotion. When you were put into bed at night, did your parent(s) tell you bedtime facts, or bedtime stories? Stories are told because they entertain, teach lessons, stir emotion, and deliver a message far better than rattling off dry facts. Stories can package facts and deliver with relevancy into people's lives. So it matters little to your success how much *you know* about your comp plan, your product details, or other specifics. What matters most is your ability to stir someone's emotions. Can you inspire someone to act?

Stories of how people have benefitted by using your product, or how their lifestyle changed by building a business in your company, is what will sell or recruit people. You want them to say, "I want those results too!" Or "I can do what they have done and change my life as well." Your stories must be relatable. If your prospect does not feel like they can get the same results or that they aren't as good as you, their lack of belief will send them walking away.

How will you motivate your team to be productive? Stories! It's what recruited them, and it is what will move them to act. Seeing and hearing stories of people getting qualified, moving up the ranks, cashing checks, earning cars, quitting jobs, going on trips, and changing their lifestyles … *these* stories are everything! *Become* a *great storyteller*. That's it. Short stories — keep them exciting and keep them coming. A great story will take on a life of its own, and will keep being told as it travels away from you like the ripples from a stone in the pond. This is word-of-mouth marketing ... so create great word of mouth ripples. Use events, conference calls, emails, and social media to get the stories out constantly.

CONGRUENCE

Have you ever felt stuck? Maybe you haven't recruited anyone in a while, and you just can't seem to break the streak of no success. This causes you to not feel like picking up the phone and getting any more rejection. You don't feel like talking about the business that day, so you don't. Can you relate?

This is *critical* for you to always remember. You cannot avoid rejection. Ninety percent of people are always going to tell you that your business is not for them. You have to go through the no's to get to the *yes*es. There is no other way around it. You may not *like* making calls and accepting no's, but you will like the results and income you *will* get by doing it consistently enough. Bank on it.

So here's what happens to everyone, myself included. You have a bad day, where everyone says no. You wake up the next day and you just cannot get yourself to make some calls. The whole day goes by and you did nothing to grow your business. The next day, you have a nagging little feeling of guilt about doing nothing the day before, so you start to internalize it. You question whether you know what you are doing. Does the business work? Is it worth the effort? You know the answer is yes, so you don't quit — but you also do no activity.

The next day, that little guilt feeling has mushroomed

even bigger. And as time goes on, the guilt turns into self-loathing. You get down on yourself for not performing like you know you could and should. You begin to beat yourself up and even compare yourself to others. Sadly, this can become a downward spiral that is self-inflicted and hard to break out of. Without being wise enough to seek direct help from an upline expert, some people never recover. Instead of fixing their mindset and bringing their goals and the actions back into alignment — getting congruent — they quit the business. These are the blamers who walk the Earth claiming the business didn't work. No! They stopped working! Don't be a blamer. Be *congruent*. Make your activity match up with your *WHY* in the business. Pick up the phone and snap back into action. Don't allow yourself to be depressed, because it *is* a form of depression. Your upline can help you snap out of it.

How do you stay congruent? Here are a few tips:

Break the ice by starting your day making three- to *four calls early in the morning.* By doing this, you will *conquer call reluctance!* It's picking up the heavy phone to make those first few calls that's the bear! By getting them done quick and early, you will feel proud of yourself and empowered versus letting the loathing and guilt from procrastination kick in again. Get those first calls made early, and see if you can spark a roll. It is also best to *plan your* *day the night before.* If you wake up without a definite plan of attack, you will likely do nothing. Write down some exact things you will accomplish at a certain time, and keep to your plan.

TWO JARS AND SOME MARBLES

Get two glass jars. On one of them, tape pictures of what you are trying to get away from (job, bills, debt, old car) and on the other tape pictures of your *why*/dreams (kids, Disney World, new car, boat, church, island trip). Then in the first "bad" jar, put in the number of marbles you intend to make phone calls or exposures for the day. Every time you make a call/exposure, transfer one marble into the "good" dream jar. Don't let your day end with-

out moving all (5, 10, 20, 30) the marbles into the good jar. This will attach your *why* to the actions of making the calls, and help you *track* your activity.

Here's another way to use jars to create *buy in* with your family. I had a couple in my business with a son and daughter. Understanding that this business required them to not be home a few times a week to attend events, they needed support from the whole family. So they asked the kids what they really wanted to do. They said they were dying to go to Disney World. So they had the kids cut out pictures of some Disney characters, and gathered in the kitchen with a big glass jar and tape. The parents explained that in order to be able to afford the trip to see Mickey, it was going to require some business meetings a few nights a week and even a weekend or two. So they taped the pictures onto the jar and promised that upon returning from every meeting away from home, they would give the kids 50 cents each to put into the jar. When the jar was full, they would buy the tickets and fly to Disney! Guess what they repeated to me one night?

"Mom and Dad? Why are you home tonight? Don't you have a meeting you can go to? We want to go to Disney this year! Go to another meeting!"

That's called awesome buy-in! Family support is wonderful if you have it. And it can be created if you don't.

WHAT REALLY DRIVES YOU?

When we talk about determining what our *why* is … it seems noble to write down and tell others that we want to succeed for our kids, to help others, or provide for our families. These are surely motivating. But I will say something right now that I have never heard anyone else say from stage in our industry: *More than those worthy and noble reasons for success we mentioned above, the biggest real driver for each of us is really EGO.*

You see, it is totally fine and healthy to have selfish reasons for wanting to win. What every human being wants in life are two main things — *love* and *respect*. These "drives" fuel everything we do, think about, and strive for.

When we say we want to be selfless and help others, we can translate that into meaning we want to do so because it makes us feel good about ourselves for doing it. This is actually selfish. You see, it is OK to have selfish drives, especially when others benefit in the process. Think about it; would you help others if it made you feel bad about yourself afterwards? No, you wouldn't. You help others to help them, but also because you know you will be proud (pride/ego) of yourself for doing so. Even the person who donates money anonymously (which shows they want no recognition for the deed) still gets to benefit knowing in their own head that they helped their fellow man. It cannot be escaped. We can talk it in circles. Bottom line, we get off on being selfless. It feeds our own ego, like it or not. So ego does play the lead role in what motivates each of us. Stop fighting it, and embrace it.

Here's another example. Someone says they are doing this business for their kid. Wow, that must really motivate them and move them to act like never before! Well, guess what? It's not really about their kid. If it were about the kid, they'd be doing much more in the business. So attaching their *why* to their kid isn't working, because although noble … it just might not be the biggest driver for them. If they get honest and admit/accept that it's OK for their *ego* to be a reason to succeed, they just might take off to new heights.

We all want to have *self-respect.* By doing the activity, even though you may dread it, you will respect yourself once you do it. You will be congruent with your goals and actions in alignment. Once you have self-respect, only then can you receive the respect of others, which is what every human longs for. Once we love ourselves, others can love us. If we don't love and respect ourselves, we are not able to accept these from anyone else.

So the way I see it, EGO = Love and Respect. A healthy ego, one that is strong yet grounded, is the backbone. You have to first have it in order to give it. So if success in your business will allow you to love and respect yourself more, you will, in turn, make the world a better place.

MOTIVATION OR ANIMOSITY

In 2001, when I was making about $400,000 a year in the third year in my company, I decided I would go buy a Ferrari. In thinking that this would drive my team to want to work towards this type of reward for themselves, I emailed them a question asking what color Ferrari I should pick. I immediately got some who answered back emphatically with their choice, and their proclamation of what color theirs will be one day.

But I was surprised to have received a very different response from one team member. He said that I was being inconsiderate to send out such an email to people who were not making as much money. So for him, he received it as a slap in his face. Maybe it caused him to confront the fact that he was not where he wanted to be in his business. He measured himself against my success as if somehow mine took away from his. It was as if he had tremendous animosity built up due to comparing himself against his upline. This is a dangerous and sabotaging mindset. If you cannot celebrate and be encouraged by the success of another, how can you expect that your success will be acceptable or motivational to your big future team?

When you see success stories in your company, embrace them. Champion them. Envision yourself having that success, and creating such success stories in your team. If you cannot have joy for others, you will not be able to have the success they have. If you are the kind of person who gets pissed off about others having success, you will never have that success. But if that success story motivates you, you will use it to build your belief and eventually have similar success yourself.

So as a leader, should I have not sent out that email? Should I have held back something that would motivate the right people who have the proper mindset that is required to win? Of course not. I cannot cater to the lowest common denominator. As leaders we have to cater to the winners, and let the others either fix their broken mindsets or shake themselves out of the business. I would much rather take the person who is making $5,000/month *and* has the right mindset, and motivate them to come get to the top.

This reminds me once again of a portion of the quote from Marianne Williamson that I mentioned in a previous chapter:

> *... as we let our own light shine, we consciously give other people permission to do the same.*

So get out there, shine your light and inspire those around you to do the same. If someone else gets jealous or insecure, you can be empathetic, but do not shrink your dream casting. If you let one person cause you to throttle back and not be so excited about your success, you will have let that one person stop you from helping countless others dream bigger and believe that they will be there one day, too.

GET PISSED OFF

When a negative naysayer tries to burst your bubble, how do you let it impact you? Do you buy into their opinion? When you buy someone else's opinion, you buy their lifestyle. Who cares what they think? Well, you know what? I cared! When people got under my skin with their negative or condescending comments, I stopped brushing it off and let it cause my blood to boil — on purpose! We often hear that we need to let our dreams and goals motivate us. That's all good. But sometimes we need an enemy to want to fight and conquer. I wanted to throw their words back in their face as I pulled a copy of my massive check out of my folder and say, "*POWWW*! Look at this, you punk!" Now I am not sure I ever did it exactly that way … but close! My own family told me I was foolish and wasting my time in this business. I let those remarks linger in my head as fuel for my fire. I made 30, 40, 50 calls a day with the intention of proving these people wrong in my mind.

It is OK to let something negative fuel us, too. So when I got that first check that was $11,405 … I faxed it to my brother. He still put it down. Six months later my check was $24,000 for the month, and again I faxed it over. His demeanor changed slightly, but he was still a bit dismissive. Six more months, and my check that month of $42,000 was put into the fax machine. I was sure to have my brother and dad waiting on the other end, since neither was very nice to me early on about this "little business I was in." I could hear their jaws drop to the floor when they saw the amount.

In the *Appendix* section of this book, I've created a document called "Your Dream's Flu Shot." This document is designed for you to hand out to every new recruit who joins your team. Your goal is to inoculate them against the naysayers, the rejection, and the urges to quit. If you do not *warn them up front* about what they will encounter as they proceed to launch their business, they could be blown out before they really even begin. If each recruit is prepared for what's coming, and know *why* they should be expecting it, they will be empowered to push right through it.

PROCRASTINATION — THE DREAM KILLER

The graveyards across the country are filled with dreams that never came true. Most of those sad souls never had the courage or the fortitude to get off the mark and just go for it in life. They had the same God-given qualities as the great success stories we have all seen on TV and read about in magazines, but they didn't have the ambitious nature to take a risk and win.

It reminds me of the story about the country house down the way with a dog yelping non-stop on the front porch. The next-door neighbor was getting very agitated because the family was not home, and they left their dog outside making so much noise. So he decided to walk over to the house to find out what the problem was with this big old dog that was howling like he wanted to be heard for miles. The neighbor approached the dog carefully and tried to calm it down, to no avail. So he finally decided to grab the dog by its collar and lead it around back. As soon as the dog stood up, the howling stopped. The neighbor was puzzled. Was that all he had to do? Get the dog up? Turns out, the dog was sitting on a nail that was protruding up from a floorboard on the porch. So why in the world did the dog not just get up and move? Well, I guess it just didn't hurt badly enough!

This story of the dog sitting on a nail rings true with countless people I have met in my networking career. People yelp, howl, and complain non-stop about how miserable their life is, how little money they have, or how stressed out they are. But yet they choose not to get up and change it! They just prefer to keep sitting on the nail and whining. My advice to you is *don't be that dog!* And don't waste time on dogs with not enough sense to get themselves up off the nail, either.

You will come across people every day who don't dream anymore. One of our jobs is to help people to dream again, and then show them a path to achieve those dreams. You will also find dreamers who have been dreaming for years, but that's about all they do. They won't do what it takes to achieve their goals, but rather they just talk about them. People generally know that they need to make changes and do something about their situation. But most just will not take action. Some will freeze due to fear of failure, fear of success, or just plain laziness. Sometimes people will put success off until a later date because in their mind they feel like they have to wait until their plate is totally clear before they put something else on it. The most successful people I have ever met were often multi-taskers who seized opportunities when they arose, not only when it was convenient. They know that they cannot choose when the right opportunities will show up, and they cannot predict if timing will ever be better. They grab on and do their best with the resources they have. And it's not really about having resources, but rather being *resourceful.*

Do not put off until tomorrow what you know you

should and *can* do today. If you procrastinate in this business of yours, it is likely becoming a part of who you are and how you operate … and it will impact all areas of your life. You can make excuses or you can make money, but you can't make both. There is nothing to wait for. You cannot wait until you have the skills, or learn everything about the business first. That's the ultimate Catch 22. You will never learn it if you don't do it. What you lack in skill, you make up in numbers. Just go through the learning curve faster, right away. Rip the bandage off and get it over with. Jump in the pool and get used to the temperature.

THE AWESOME POWER OF AFFIRMATIONS

What is your self-talk? Are you positive or negative? Do you sow seeds of belief into yourself, or seeds of doubt?

Thoughts are things. What you think about often manifests into your life. If you keep thinking about how tired you are, you'll get more tired. If you think about illness, you will bring on sickness. If you dwell on failure, you will attract more failure. You attract what you think about. So if you accept and understand this, you can change the course of your life and business by doing the opposite. Think about being healthy, you can ward off sickness. Think about and expect success, and you will succeed.

Now don't mistake this to mean you can sit around thinking everything into happening. No! Too many people do nothing but think and dream, and act little on the positive thoughts. Think right, then speak it into existence alongside the proper actions required to win.

What is an "affirmation?" You decide what it is that

you want, and then you put it into a first person, present declaration. Then you repeat it to yourself constantly. For example, let's say you want to be the top position in your company (let's call it Platinum). You will say to yourself every day, "I am a Platinum!" You say it with *belief* and enthusiasm. If you just say it and don't believe it as you say it, you are wasting your time. Sell yourself on the idea, then write the affirmation, then repeat it five times daily without fail.

CONCEIVE IT → *BELIEVE* IT → *ACHIEVE* IT

Here are a few ideas to start.

- I am a top recruiter

- I am a fearless leader

- People want to work with me

- I am a warrior for freedom

- I am a great sponsor/coach

- I am living my dream

- I am changing thousands of lives

- I am a great speaker

- I am building the fastest growing team

You can read my personal daily affirmation in the *Appendix* section of this book.

S.O.S. — SHINY OBJECT SYNDROME

The good thing about people who join your business is that they had to be open-minded to check it out and get started. The same holds true for you. So respect the open mind, because without it, you would not be in the business you are today. But I must share this *warning*, and you should also be sure your team understands this as well.

Once you have evaluated your business, done your due diligence, and started your business, do *not falter*! Do not look right and left. There is no need to look at other opportunities. You will inevitably be pitched all kinds of network marketing businesses now that you are a marketer. Likely you will come across some very slick-talking, hype-casting characters who will do all they can to convince you that you are in the wrong company. They will try to get you to believe their business is so much better. They will flaunt stories of the big money people are making and make you believe if you switch and come over it will happen for you, too. And if they catch you in a period where you are not yet succeeding the way you desire, you might be attracted to their sales pitch. This is called the "Shiny Object Syndrome."

In my many years in network marketing, I have watched countless people who fell for the latest shinier object that came their way. I call them "bouncers" or "MLM junkies." They jump from deal to deal, trying to be first or early in the game. This, in my experience, is a very bad way to approach a business career. I have seen this wreck people financially, as well as destroy their credibility and relationships.

Here's what you need to remember. You are smart. You made the decision to start the business because you saw the value in the product/service personally. You saw documentation that there is significant money being made by many people in the business already. If they can succeed with the same product, comp plan, and tools — so can you! Those successful people likely gave it time and focus that you have yet to put forth. But when you learn what they have learned, and do what they have done … you will get the same kind of results. It's called the "You Factor." Everyone in your business is working with the same product and the same comp plan. The only difference is *you*.

So don't even engage in conversation or in exploration online of the many other businesses out there. What good will that serve you? All it can do is confuse your mind, and cause you to question if you are in the right place. If you invested your money and opened a few McDonald's restaurants, would you take calls from Wendy's or Pizza Hut to hear about why you should fold it up and open some of their stores instead? Of course you would not let that junk into your headspace.

People are often prone to fall for something *new*. You hear about someone cheating on the spouse they love. Why? The "newness" of that other person showing them attention catches their eye, like a shiny object. How often does that turn out well? You chose your mate because you loved their qualities. Will it always be the way it was when you first started dating? No, for sure. But how would your life be if you dropped out of the relationship after the newness wore off and you see another good-looking person? I bet that would lead to a pretty unfulfilled life, kind of shallow. Or how about when the exciting newness of your business wears off and a fresh new business comes onto your radar screen? The countless "jumpers" I have known in the network market industry have some things in common. They are often broke, desperate to find a new financial fix, and not living happy lives. They are void of the enrichment that comes from making a decision, having commitment to a vision, and seeing their plan to completion and success.

I spoke at a generic MLM training symposium last year, as one of a dozen speakers from different companies. When the host introduced me, he shared that I have been with my company for 14 years. The audience literally gasped out loud. I saw people looking at each other in semi-disbelief. It was amazing to them that a networker was building one business for that long! It really baffles me that this should be so uncommon. I would think everyone would want to find a place to call home, build it once, and have it stick so that they can get paid on that effort for the rest of their life. I wouldn't want to be jumping from deal to deal, always having to rebuild. That's not fun. It's risky and destroys credibility. When will you ever feel secure and be able to go on cruise control to enjoy the residuals that you built?

So next time you are tempted to pull over on the side of the road you're on to see what that shiny object is, I hope you will decide to put on your sunglasses and keep looking straight ahead. Have commitment, have faith, and be confident in the decision you made when you began your business.

YOU CAN LEAD A HORSE TO WATER ...

"You can lead a horse to water, but you can't force it to drink." We have all heard this statement a thousand times. And it is very true. If the horse doesn't want to drink, it won't. Just like if you recruit someone into your business, and can't make him or her do the activity to build it. I know this is a very common frustration for us as builders. How can someone see the opportunity, pay good money to start the business ... then do nothing? It's ridiculous. But it is reality. So is there anything that can be done? The answer is *yes*, you absolutely can do something about it!

So how do you make a horse drink the water? Remember, the horse is only going to do what it *wants* to do. So instead of thinking you can force it to drink ... you need to *convince* the horse that it is thirsty so it *wants* to drink on its own! How do you do this? I bet if you feed it some dry grass, it might get dry-mouth and want to drink water. Or maybe if you show it other horses that are drinking water, your horse might feel like maybe it ought to be doing what it sees others doing.

Let's relate this now to convincing your recruits to actually do the business. So you led them to the business, they signed up, and then won't budge. You need to convince them that doing activity is what *they* want to do, not what *you* want them to do. This is done by showing them that they are thirsty for change. What is the equivalent of feeding the dry grass to a horse? Feed them a picture of their reality. Actually connect with them to learn about their life. Find out what might be missing or in need of change. If you can help them realize what they lack in time freedom, or that their kids rarely see them, or that they are living in financial scarcity … they will now start to feel a thirst to change what they might not have paid conscious attention to previously.

The second strategy, which is akin to showing the horse *other* horses drinking water, works well, too. This means you keep parading success stories of other distributors in front of your recruit so they see that others just like them are doing it and succeeding — so they can too! Recruits don't like to do as they are told, and they won't. They like to do what they *want* to do. Seeing other people they can relate to doing activity and getting results will move them into action far better than you insisting that they work it. I usually spend my efforts in promotion. I will promote for my recruits to attend briefing and training events so they can see the other horses drinking water. I will promote for them to hear the stories on conference calls. I will urge them to watch DVDs with testimonials, or to be active followers on Facebook to see the flow of success stories.

If you are successful in getting a horse to drink water once, that does not mean it will always keep drinking it. The next time you lead it to water, you may need to coax it again using the above methods. Oftentimes, it will take many cycles through this routine to develop a healthy drinking habit for the horse. This is totally true for your downline. You are the leader. You cannot let yourself get so frustrated when your people require continual coaxing. You might find yourself considering quitting on your own dreams and goals if this frustration persists. Just know that it is a natural part of this business, just as it is with the horses. You cannot get mad at the horse, or it will spite you and make you walk home. If you get mad at your recruits, they will feel your bad energy and quit the business and leave the empire you are building.

Just keep in mind that it is natural for your new recruits to require the convincing and coaxing. Would you stop coaxing the one-year-old baby you are trying to teach to take her first steps and learn to walk? I would hope not. As a parent, you know that it's just a matter of sticking with it and the baby will soon catch on and walk on her own two feet. Your recruits, in time, will also catch on if you don't guilt them into feeling bad and quitting first. It is a delicate balance of coaching, understanding, and empathy.

If one method or tactic does not motivate them to act, try another, then another. Don't give up on finding the magic formula for that person. Every person will have a unique *something* that motivates him or her. For some, it's simply a matter of convincing them they are thirsty by pointing out what's wrong in their life that they can fix. For others, it might be the need to be inspired by seeing people who are doing better than they are. Our job is to recruit folks, but the real job starts once they are recruited. And this is the most rewarding part of our business — when we take someone under our wing and teach them to fly. I have had very few instances where my recruit came on board and began flying right off the bat. Most every one of my superstars took weeks or months of coddling, hand-holding, coaching, and promoting. But I can attest to you that the time investment pays off in a big way. So recruit and stay with them until you learn their hot buttons … then watch them start drinking the water on their own!

7

Modeling Your Empire

WHAT SEPARATES TOP EARNERS FROM AVERAGE NETWORKERS

Why are there only a select few who become the mega stars in sports, entertainment, music, arts, or business? I believe it is because there are only a few who select themselves to truly pursue mastery of their craft. They are relentless in their practicing. They have a dogged determination to be the best, not just to be good. They shudder at the thought of being good. When those who are "good" rest after a long day, the masters continue to burn the candle.

Tiger Woods became the best golfer in the world by spending years of his life hitting buckets and buckets of balls, then playing rounds of golf, then hitting more buckets. Golf was his calling. He made it his life focus. Due to this focus, his rise to the top paved the way to renaissance the game of golf. Tiger made kids around the world want to pick up a golf club and learn the game.

Michael Jordan wanted to play basketball. Getting cut from his high school team ignited a fire inside of him to prove to the world he could play with the best. His ambition for greatness made him the best. He missed more than

9,000 shots in his career, lost almost 300 games, missed 26 game-winning shots, failed over and over … and that's why he succeeded. Jordan never stopped working on himself, and he never forgot getting cut from that team.

Steve Jobs was a great example in the business realm. He was never satisfied with anything short of perfection. He held tight to his convictions, even to the point of being forced out of the company he founded. But he came back to create an Apple that changed how the world connects and communicates, making it the most valuable company on the planet. Not everything Steve touched was a success. But he was always in the zone — focused on his mission. Steve would not be satisfied with an iPhone just being a good phone. He pursued greatness, in every way. His legacy will long outlive him.

Top million-dollar earners in network marketing are very much the same as the examples above. You can make a living in networking if you are good at it, and work hard at it. But to become legendary, you have to not just "work *in* the business." You also have to "work *on* the business." Working *in* it means you are doing the activity — selling product and recruiting. This is what I call "Phase One" activity. The masters are in Phase One constantly. They keep their axe sharp. But working *on* your business means you are creating team culture, developing leaders, cultivating relationships, solving problems, scaling the expansion, looking for growth opportunities, and ensuring The System is running effectively. Also included in this is working on yourself.

"How can I become better?" To become a master, here are some things that you will need to focus on:

- Speaking ability

- Motivating and leading

- Creating leaders by empowering people

- Storytelling

- Living a life others want to model

- Keeping the business simple

I have a saying that I have been pounding on the table for years: "Stay on the Elevator." We all get on the elevator and ride it up to different floors of income. Some people get off on the first floor at $1,000/month. Some stay on by keeping doing the same Phase One (selling and recruiting) activity until the doors open on the $2,000/month floor, and they get off. Some stay on until they get to the floor at $4,000. Some ride it up to $10K. Some to $20K. Some to $100K. But eventually, just about everyone "gets off the elevator." This means at some point, they stop doing what got them to that level. When they stop doing it, their team follows their example and they stop doing it also. This causes the team to go backwards. That is why I have always stayed on the elevator. I want to lead my team by example. They will do what they see, not what you say. Now at some point, when you are ready to slow down (when your income is beyond need, and you have accomplished all of your goals), you will be able to. But only after you have duplicated yourself by creating more leaders like you, and have empowered them to carry the torch of influence with their teams into the future.

So the key to becoming a top earner is identifying your Rising Stars, and pouring your time into their development. You can only handle doing this with one- to three people at a time. Just like a golf coach can only focus on one or two golfers. Decide who deserves your focus and then determine if they're willing to commit 100 percent to being developed. Your goal is to help them master Phase One, and then teach them how to become a leader. Once this leader is developed, then the final step is to teach him/her how to identify Rising Stars and mentor them in this same way. You want to create a "Leader Factory."

Top Earners think bigger, walk bigger, talk bigger, and most importantly, act bigger. They have bigger goals, work more hours, and put more heart and energy into those hours. They are present, enthusiastic, and bold. They see this business as their calling, and as a way to serve others.

If you help enough others get what they want, you will get all that you want and more. Be a *servant leader*. focus on the goals of those you serve, and less on your own goals. Your own goals will be limited by what you alone can accomplish. But by leveraging the accomplishment of the goals of many people on your team … their goals will boost your personal rewards far beyond what you could ever achieve by focusing on just yourself.

GOAL SETTING

Goal setting is critical to your success. I learned years ago from Billionaire Paul J. Meyer (search him online) how important goals are — and how big of a part they played in my journey. People with no goals are going nowhere. Goals give you a purpose to focus on, and they fuel your fire to do the necessary activity to accomplish them.

Goals must have *all* of these traits to be effective:

1. Meaningful

2. Specific

3. Written

4. Shared

5. Time line attached

6. Reward upon completion

I spent so many nights and mornings dwelling on my goals. I made sure my goals had deep-rooted meaning to my life. I made sure they were crystallized in my brain and very concise. I wrote them down everywhere, so I could see them often. I shared them with my family and with my team. I made sure that they were not open-ended, but rather had clear deadlines to accomplish them. And lastly, I set up rewards for myself to make it all worth the effort.

Now, just because I am not elaborating more on this topic, please do not let this subject die here. Paul J. Meyer and other good authors have incredible books on this topic.

TREAT IT LIKE A BUSINESS

Treat it like a business and it will pay you like a business. Treat it like a hobby, it will cost you like a hobby.

Too many, almost all, network marketers do not treat this like a real business. To most, it is something they are trying out to see if maybe they can make some extra money. This whole sense of "trying out" to "see if" is the culprit for the failure most people attract. They quit because they never committed in the first place! You get out of this business model what you put into it. If you give it 10 percent of your time, energy, and focus, you cannot get mad and say the business doesn't work. *It works, if you work it.* If your expectations are not in alignment with your actions, then you will certainly set yourself up for disappointment.

I can assure you, because I have seen it thousands of times, if you treat your business as if you invested $1 million of your hard-earned money to start it, you will find a way to win! The problem is that most network marketing businesses cost less than $500 to start. So with little skin in the game, it is far too easy to nickel and dime it. Thus, you earn nickels and dimes.

So what does it mean to "treat it like a business?"

1. *Commit to attending events consistently.* This is like having a store and going in to open the doors for your customers consistently.

2. *Be a regular on conference calls.* Be a perpetual learner, always trying to improve and get better results.

3. *Track.* You want to track your activities, as well as your results. If certain activities are not yielding the desired results, then you can review to find appropriate improvements.

4. *Investment.* It takes money to make money. You may need to buy tools/materials, generate traffic to your site, or buy leads. If you are running a downline sales force, you might decide to offer incentives or contests to stimulate them.

5. *Learn from defeat.* You will not always win. Learn from mistakes, and get better next time. Be willing to grow through your learning curve.

6. *Treat your customers with love and respect.* This is referring to your actual customers, as well as your distributors (they are also in a way your customers).

7. *Protect your house.* Do not let anyone tarnish your company brand or your image. Make sure everyone is operating with integrity, never misleading the consumer or the team. Report unacceptable behavior to the company for review.

8. *Every distributor is a distribution point for your business.* Do all that you can to keep them plugged in, productive, and positive.

9. *Pay your taxes.* You are a 1099 independent contractor/business owner. Therefore, income taxes are not withheld. It is up to you to calculate how much money you should put aside for taxes. And after your first year having developed earnings history, you will need to make estimated quarterly tax payments going forward. So seek a tax advisor.

THE ULTIMATE DAY — MY TYPICAL DAY

As I thought I was done writing and this book was all wrapped up, one of my networking friends asked me for some coaching. His request was for me to outline for him what my day looked like when I was building at my best, when I went full-time. This is a great question, because in reality, most full-timers are barely working their business the way they should. Just because they no longer have a job does not mean they are working this business full-time. Here is my answer to him … which, by the way, I *still* operate like this to this very day.

9 a.m. — I wake up with an energy drink. I don't drink coffee, but I have healthy alternatives. I will also do a quick breakfast and lots of water. To get charged up, I read about 15-20 minutes of personal development material. This material is not heavy, but usually consists of books on attitude, thinking big, energy, focus, etc. I ask myself, "If my downline does what I do today, how much money will I be making?" This reminds me to do what I want my team to do!

9:30 a.m. — I start off by making IPA (income producing activity) calls to prospects right away. I want to break the ice as early in the morning as possible. This is *critical*, as it helps me avoid call reluctance. If I don't do this, noon can roll around and I have wasted the entire morning making no progress or income. So anywhere between three to five calls right away launches me into having a productive day.

11 a.m. — After making a number of initial prospecting calls and follow-ups on existing prospects, I will start replying back to emails and returning voicemails. I prioritize these, and some will get returned late at night during non-productive time. I will also shift gears to make a few calls to promote something to members of my team. I might be calling them to urge their attendance on a conference call or to come to an upcoming event. I will also reach out to brand new recruits on my team to welcome them, paint the vision, and to help book their PBR and PCC. Throughout the day, I also take a number of three-way calls from my team to close their prospects.

My focus will shift around throughout the day from calling my own prospects, to calling my team members, or to taking three-way calls. Of course, there may be a webinar to conduct, or a sit-down appointment to meet with someone in person. Here again is the diagram of what that time allocation will often look like:

TIME	
25% Contacting my own new prospects to recruit	**25%** Following up on my own existing prospects on my list
Doing three-way calls/third-party closes for my team **25%**	Calling my team to promote something and inspire action **25%**

I try to have an event of some kind to do in the evening. This might be speaking at a PBR, or at a briefing, or conducting some PCCs from home. If I am driving to do an event outside of my home, I use my drive time wisely and productively. I will print out a list of prospects and team members to call while heading down the road. If I have 30 minutes in the car to and from, that gives me an hour to squeeze in an extra 20-30 dials. I love this much more than listening to the radio. If I need a break, I will listen to some PD (personal development) or training CDs. But I try to reserve this listening for non-productive hours. If it is time that I can be making calls, I want to be making them.

For lunch or dinner — If I am not with family and eating alone, I have a pen and pad to jot down and brainstorm ideas. I love to be creative and always thinking of ways to help the team, or ways to create more business. Sometimes I will pick up a book and read while eating. The more I read, the better I get. But I only read when I cannot be talking on the phone.

At the end of my night (by 9:30 p.m., unless I have a late conference call or PCC for the West Coast), I will wind ·down with a light snack and stretch. I might watch some TV, but often will get 10-20 more pages of a PD book. As I brush my teeth, I ask myself, "If my downline did what I did today, how much money would I be making?" Again, it causes me to assess my own performance for the day.

As Jim Rohn once said, "The sleep of a laboring man is sweet." When I go to bed, I like to know I left it all out on the field that day. My self-esteem is high when I know I gave it my all. Can you imagine if you put in a *full day* like me, how you would feel about yourself? And how your business would explode?

One more thing as far as time management: Schedule your down time just as much as you schedule your time for business. When you are an ambitious person like me, you can get into a rhythm and be laser focused on business. You might be thinking about your business constantly, and trying to work it all the time. So it is imperative that you remember that you have other priorities in your life too. So just like you block out time for building your business, you need to schedule time to spend with your spouse, with your kids, and even your friends. Don't neglect your business, and don't neglect them. I have mostly taken Fridays off after 2 p.m. This is my personal time for nurturing friendships, and keeping fun in my life. If I do not have a big event that weekend for my business, Saturdays are often my down day. In the beginning, I built seven days a week for a while until my momentum was cranking. But then I got balance back. It was worth getting unbalanced for a bit. Now I live any way I wish.

Family time is blocked out each day, as well as my time to work out and stay in shape physically. I also take an awesome vacation every three months or so, and leave the country at least twice a year. Basically, I *design* my *own life.* I map out the way I want my life lived … and then I wrap my business around it. I created balance, even though it took work and lack of balance for a period. It is worth it!

8

The Builder's Actions and Behaviors

JOURNAL YOUR JOURNEY (SO YOU CAN TELL YOUR STORY ONCE YOU'VE MADE IT)

One thing I wish I did much more than I had, is journaling everything that I experienced along the way. I had so many ups and downs, cheers and cries, wins and defeats. I just wish I created a diary that I could open up to the world and let you see what it took for me to grow in this business (and in life). If I could show you pictures or video footage of me from when I entered network marketing, and then show you the same footage every three years, you might be amazed. We can never really see our own metamorphosis as the days tick by. But in hindsight, the lessons I learned seem to all blend together and only a few stand out. But they all have combined into the recipe that has made me a very humbly, successful person. I can see certain things now as I pause my life to sit and reflect in order to write this book for you. And going forward, it is my intent to be even more present and fully take in every experience that life leads me into. I will savor those personal conversations and connections with my team members. I will write down the lessons I learned from specific defeats as I encounter them.

Go ahead with your career in network marketing journaling every experience, so that when your time comes to write a book about how you built a team bigger than mine — it will almost already be written. Take lots of pictures. Shoot videos. Document it all. Live your life like it is a movie, with your favorite soundtrack playing in the background. You are the star, and your teammates are the co-stars. Take the lead role and nail it!

BE LIKE AN ANT

Have you ever watched ants? The little bugs are rather admirable. They have the ability to target exactly where they are going, and they find a way to get there. You can see them walk in a line towards their goal. But if you place a block between them and the goal, do they decide that this obstacle is too large to overcome and turn back? No ... it doesn't matter what you try to do to block their path, they find a way! They will go over, under, or around until they accomplish their mission. Ants are relentless and unstoppable.

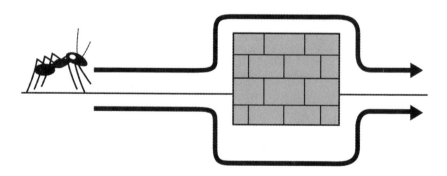

That's the way networkers have to be. Pick your goal, and then be like an ant. Determination is the common characteristic of all seven-figure earners in network marketing. Don't let the fake stories of luck fool you. Every millionaire got there with dedicated work ethic. They put blinders on and kept their heads down and moved forward. Ants don't seem to get upset when you try to block their path. They don't even slow down. They just keep charging on until they succeed. So can you. *Develop an ant mentality ... nothing is going to stop you!*

ESP

"I quit because my upline never helped me."

How many times have I heard that over the last 15 years? Oh, my gosh! I must admit how frustrating it can be working with people. We all start our network marketing business as independent business owners, 1099 independent contractors. What happens with it is up to us. We get out of this business what we put into it. We all get introduced to, and brought into the company, by a sponsor. Their goal is to bring us in and be the best sponsor they know how to be.

The reality is that most people are novices themselves, and do not know how to be a good sponsor. They may have only been in the business days or weeks themselves. But everyone has more people with more knowledge upline from them. If someone wants to succeed, they *must* learn to follow the chain up the line to find someone who is successful in the business and willing to help them. It may be the person five or 10 levels above them. It may even take some phone work to track down a good mentor up the chain … but it is worth finding the right support.

When people complain that I never called to help them, I try to explain that I do not have ESP. I cannot read their minds and know exactly when they need my help. My phone takes all incoming calls. Somehow people think that I should know when they are struggling, or when they have a question, or that they are sitting there waiting on a phone call. To me that's just plain odd! If I were in their shoes, and really wanted to succeed, I would pick up my phone and call for help. But that's just me. I consider myself an ambitious self-starter. Maybe that's why I succeed while others fail. Sorry to sound so blunt, but come on! To all my friends and fellow networkers reading this book — please, *today,* reach out to the full-time and most successful people upline from you and lock arms with them. Explain to them your *why,* outline your commitment of actions you plan to take, and set expectations on how you can utilize them for help. Your upline has no clue that you are even thinking about this business. They don't have ESP either. But I assure you that they will light up to hear from you — that you are ready to rock and roll!

POSITIVE DOWN, NEGATIVE UP

This is a very emotional business, because it's a people business. And when people are involved, you will inevitably have problems. Our job as leaders is to constantly make sure that everyone on the team is focused and positive. We have to protect the fragile psyche of every single person in the downline. All it takes is one problem to come up, and it could knock that person right out of the business. The problem might not even be theirs, but one that they *heard* others talking about. In the word of mouth industry we are in, good news travels fast, but bad news flies at Mach 10!

How do we control the psychological environment within our teams for success? Find every reason to pass positive communications *down* to the team constantly. Get everyone doing this. You can speak excitement and belief into existence. People are attracted to positive people who like to uplift the spirit of others. As leaders, people are watching everything we do, and listening to everything we say. So if you have nothing good to say, say nothing. I have *never* witnessed a complainer, gossiper, or negative person make it to the top in network marketing. Only the positive leaders are able to attract and retain, and build winning teams. With everything that comes at us in life, do what I do and take in constant, daily doses of personal development books and CDs to keep me in the positive zone.

Any time there is an issue or anything negative that needs to be dealt with, it must *only* go *upline*. Do not spread poison onto your people. Your upline is the only person you should bring your problems to. If you ever take it down to your team, this can, and will, cause the team to stop being productive and focus on your "stuff" instead. Here's an important question: Why would you want to bring down the morale of people under you? When you do that, it hurts *your* income! So there is *never* a valid reason to do so. The only time you talk about an issue with someone else other than your upline mentor is when you are addressing the source of the problem.

My mentor used to say, "Never pee in your swimming pool." What I would add to that is that we must also be the lifeguard who also doesn't let *anyone* else pee in the pool we are all swimming in. We all have to take responsibility for protecting our house. We get what we focus on. So be extremely conscious about creating a positive environment that people are attracted to.

MANAGING YOUR CONTACTS

Building our contact list is critical. Your list is your goldmine, and you should be adding prospects to it daily. The more people you have in your pipeline, the more will come out the other end as a part of your team. Wealthy people build networks, while everyone else looks for work. Most people see that as referring to the people who are in your downline. But I also believe your prospect database is also a network … and a very valuable one.

How are you managing this list? Are you old fashioned and keeping their contact info and notes on each person in notebooks? Or are you using an online platform (CRM) to manage this database and keep it all in one place, accessible from any computer anywhere you are? There are some simply amazing systems/platforms out there now that will not only enable you to never lose another contact, but will help you enhance the way you use your database. You can take notes on your conversations, set alarms to remind you to make follow up calls, send auto-responder drip emails to them, and even integrate an online presentation that tracks what they review. Such systems allow you to automate your business building efforts, saving you time and even working *for* you while you sleep or go on vacation. My team uses such a system, and I can direct anyone to where/how to set up this platform.

However you choose to manage your contacts, it all comes back to the premise that the *fortune is in the follow-up*. A database or list that is never worked is one that you might as well not have spent the time and money amassing. Of course, we get more excited looking for the next new prospect. But remember that there is gold in the mine we already have in that list. Who can you get on the phone and call today that you have been procrastinating on?

STOP! Put this book down and go make calls to three of them now. Feel the mental breakthrough in doing so!

AVOID END-OF-MONTH CRUNCH

In my company's business model, we operate on a monthly basis. On top of the daily commissions, people qualify each month for incentives, rank advancements, and bonuses. As you might imagine, when the month is nearing the end, people get more urgent and scramble to get customers, recruits, or points for qualifications. The final 48 hours is when people put in 25 percent of the month's business.

Here is how this can hurt your business if you are not careful.

Let's say you need to sign up customers. If you call with urgency and put pressure on prospects to buy due to your deadline, they may feel turned off by your pressuring them. Same thing happens with recruiting in this fashion. It can be dangerous in getting aggressive like this, as you might just turn off those prospects forever and *never* sign them up.

You can also turn off your team in the same way. If your downline gets more calls from you in the final few days than all month long, they will likely figure out that you are calling them because of your needs ... not to help them in hitting their goals. The last thing you want is for your team to question whether you care more about yourself than them. Conversely, if you make it your priority to work with your team with a focus on their goals all month long, they will know you care about them. Should you call them in the month-end crunch, be sure you aim your urgency towards helping them to qualify for *their* incentives. If the company is designed right, their production and success will contribute towards your qualification and success.

What I always try to remind my leaders is that I see how hard they push in the final 48 hours each month. What if they would just focus that hard in the *first* 48 hours of the month, and create that momentum early on? Instead, what I sometimes see is this huge rally on the 31st, and then the 1st they relax and catch a breather. They lose the momentum they were just creating. It is that herky-jerky, speed-up-and-stop routine that rarely gains long term traction. A smooth flow all month long starting with a burst in the beginning is always better. And you refrain from the dangerous activity of pressuring prospects or downline to make up ground each month. So get in the habit of setting goals and creating contests that are focused on the first week to 10 days of each month.

SCHOLARSHIP METHOD

So your prospect says they are very interested in the business, but they just cannot come up with the startup money. What do you do? If you tell them to call you back when they get the funds, you may hear back from 5 percent of them. If you keep on them with follow-up calls for the next few weeks or months, you may get 25 percent of them on board. But what about the 75 percent who drift away, never to join you?

The "Scholarship" method is your fallback option — your *last resort* only. Here's what you do: If you have explored all options and the person just has no way to get the money to start, get them into activity *as if* they have joined. As you know, that person is not the end … they are the means to reaching 100 people in their warm market. What is our goal? The goal is to get our message in front of every human we can come in contact with.

I would say, "OK, since there is no conceivable way for you to come up with the money to start, I will scholarship you. Here's how it works. We fill out your application and I will have it on standby. We will begin the business as if you are processed. Once we do a PBR and/or PCC and you have people signing up, we will take those commissions that are generated to pay for your entry. This way you have nothing to lose, and all to gain. And you will see the business working for you. But be sure to treat the business like you do have the money invested and skin in the game, otherwise you will not find the success that you seek. The startup cost is not the focus — it's the amount of potential earnings and change of life that you should be fired up about."

Once I have their list, or start sharing my business with their prospects, I am in control. If they flake out and still decide not to join, I can just go ahead and recruit those contacts myself. I am a networker, and I will network through my new recruits as well as those who do not join. Everyone is a doorway, and I will leave no doorways unexplored!

WARNING — If you jump to the Scholarship program too soon (before you have exhausted every option for them to find the money on their own), you will have fewer people joining legitimately with skin in the game. Your recruiting will go down. So recruit every person you can the direct way, and use this method as a last resort when you are convinced you will lose this prospect (and their contacts) otherwise.

NETWORKING GROUPS

I will combine the idea of "slow down to speed up" with quality versus quantity here. As a big recruiter for years, I have worked the numbers game. The more exposures to new prospects, the more recruits I would bring on board. When I was working part-time at first, I squeezed in 20 calls a day to opportunity seeker leads. When I went full-time, I was able to ramp up that number much higher. But often the professionals who get into our business do not want to sit at home making phone calls. Neither do the social butterflies.

Recruiters who are more interested in personal relationships and building with like-minded professionals in their local community are often drawn to another approach. Rather than calling 20-50 strangers a day, they will look for ways to slow down, physically get in front of people to build rapport, and initiate relationships. Networking groups are a common way to do this, as they are filled with business people and entrepreneurs. If you find one of these groups and they let you into their circle, you get the chance to start new friendships. From these new friendships, if formed properly without a blatant attempt for mere personal gain, you can find lots of new customers (and even recruits).

While the numbers game might lead you towards attending 20 networking/social events to meet and greet, let's analyze this. So you meet 10 new people at these social functions. By attending 20 of them, you have met 200 people. That's a big *quantity*, but most often these connections are very loose and casual, with follow-through often lacking. This is usually a hit-and-run method, unless you are truly a master networker with amazing follow-up to book appointments with these new contacts.

Joining a networking group is much different. Yes, you are meeting new people, but it is structured. You are going to be meeting with the same people every week or every month. This repetition forces the relationships to mature and become trusting, mutually beneficial partnerships. You are going in with the "Go Giver" mentality of helping them find customers for *their* business, and in turn they are helping find prospects for yours.

If you understand that slowing down to foster solid *quality* relationships/partnerships is beneficial to your long-term growth, this approach is incredible. Remember, you want to put the needs and growth of *their* business first, before you start asking for them to be your customer or send you referrals. Be selfless and be concerned about their success, and yours will surely follow naturally.

Note: Networking groups are not to be a recruiting approach. This will turn off everyone in the group and you will be shunned. While you may have someone ask about doing the business with you from time to time once they see the value in what you are selling, that is not your intent. Your goal is to market your brand, your product/service. Obviously not every product will fit every kind of group. If they are all professionals, this approach only works if you have something of value to bring to professionals.

The great thing about being in networking groups is that you will brand yourself as *the* go-to person in your town, in your circle, for what it is that you market. If people get to know you, like you, trust you, and they have a positive experience with you and your product/service, you will have business coming *to* you regularly. So focus on selling *you*, not your product, at first. Ask yourself, "How can I be of value or service to the members and their businesses?"

SUPPORT — SPOUSE AND FAMILY

Support on the home front, both emotionally and physically, is important. It makes this business journey a whole lot easier if you have it. They can be there to lift you up on your down days, which you will have. They can high-five you to celebrate your victories. They can be understanding when you have to be out at night for briefings, away for conventions, or even taking phone calls outside of a restaurant. Or they can *not* be — which makes this endeavor very taxing.

So the key is getting the *buy-in* from those in your circle. The way to do this is to paint the picture of what's in it for them. Share what the success from this business will provide for them … more money to afford nicer cars, private schools, college tuition, exotic travels, new clothes, etc. Or maybe it's the ability to retire you or your spouse from the *JOB* and have more time together for the family. Everyone must have something to gain for the support to be offered. And you must always keep painting this picture and reselling the idea constantly.

It is incumbent upon you to perform! Do what you say

you are going to do. If you make promises that your business will deliver these results, then see to it that it does. Your family is buying into your vision, your commitment, and work ethic. But if you do not do what is required to succeed, it is *your* fault. They will have every right to be angry and impatient. After all, they are giving you the latitude and free time to pursue this. Maybe they are sacrificing relationship time with you, or even watching the kids at home. The sacrifice and support they are providing needs to yield results.

So you are not just in this business for you, but also for all who are in support roles. Therefore, you better be coachable, have a burning desire, and *do* the work. If you are not making your follow-up calls, you are cheating your family. If you are not talking to sharp people when you are out, you are letting down those you care most about. Your *why* should encapsulate this, and drive you to do the work and perform — every day! Don't get surprised and feel like your family does not love and support you if they express their concern when you are not doing the required activity and bringing home the results.

Find ways to show your appreciation on a regular basis to your support network. Flowers to the wife, nice dinners out with *no phone*, romantic getaways for a weekend, fun excursions with the kids at off-times when people with jobs can't normally go. *Show* your family the *benefits* of being in this business. They need to *see* it and feel it.

FOCUS ON THE STARFISH

One day a lady was walking down the beach by the water. She looked down where the waves were washing up and she saw piles of starfish lying in the sun. She bent down and picked one up and studied it. She noticed that it was starting to dry out and was barely moving. So she threw it back into the ocean. She began to throw them in one after another. A man walked up to her and said, "Why are you bothering throwing those starfish back in? Look around; there are thousands of them washed up. You can't possibly have an impact and save them all!" She looked at him, holding up the starfish in her hand for him to see, and said, "While that may be true, I will impact *this one's* life!" Then she proceeded to throw that starfish back into the water.

My good friend just reminded me of this story as I was writing these words. He pointed out to me that he has been watching me doing the same thing with respect to my business. What he said almost brought tears to my eyes, because it really is how I feel. He repeated this story of the lady and the starfish, and said, "Brian, you do the same with each person that you pour yourself into with your business. Sure, you won't be able to save everyone or change every life … but you *can* and *will* change the one in your hand that you are working with."

This made me feel that all of my efforts, all of the time devoted to trying to impact so many lives is all worth it as long as I impact just a few. Because if I do, and that story gets told, then others will soon believe that they, too, can succeed. And if I can begin that ripple effect of belief, then my efforts will mean something. My goal is always to have a lasting impact, one that reaches well beyond my reach and my presence. So I remind myself not to be overwhelmed by the countless starfish (distributors) who may not let me throw them back into the water, and just focus on the one in my hand.

Closing Thoughts

As we close our time together in these pages, I just ask that you believe in your mission here. When people believe that *you* believe — that's when you will attract others and success can manifest in your life. Always know that *I believe in you beyond your circumstances.* We all start where we are, and grow from there. The further you have to come, the more impressive and inspirational your story will be for others, As Jim Rohn always said, "Don't wish for things to get easier … just wish for *you* to become better." Stay a student forever. When you are done growing, you begin dying. So as you go forth to learn and earn, I, too, plan to take my growth to unseen levels. Our network marketing profession needs many more leaders who embody the right philosophies and integrity to lead the way for those who have yet to even discover our better way of life.

I worked hard for years, building my business so that I can build my life. I can call all of my shots now. That's a special feeling. I made sacrifices and worked harder than most to make this my reality. Now I get to live it. And better than that, I can pay it forward and show others how to do the same. Few will do it because most won't pay the price. I don't care … some will!

In the end, what matters most to me is not how many copies of this book are sold, or getting praise for its contents. The real measurement of success will be how many readers go on to become top earners in their businesses and leaders of empire teams. When I hear that this manual was at the center of your daily journey to the pinnacle of your success, that will be the ultimate reward for the investment I made into the book. Just my name in your testimonial means more to me than the millions of dollars I have earned personally from network marketing.

Take me with you as a Foster Mentor, and we will build your empire together.

APPENDIX

QUOTES FROM THE INDUSTRY

The following quotes have been a source of inspiration for myself and for countless others in our industry. They come from a variety of sources including Jim Rohn, Anthony Robbins, Zig Ziglar, Robert Kiyosaki, Napoleon Hill, Robert Frost, myself, and others. Commit them to memory and you'll see how they will pop up again and again to give you a dose of encouragement when you need it the most.

It's not the blowing of the winds, but rather the set of the sail, that determines your destination.

If my downline did what I did today, how much money would I be making?

The magic happens when you get a large number of people, doing a few simple things, consistently over an extended period of time.

Some will, some won't. So what? Next!

Your urgency must defeat their procrastination.

If you will help enough others to get what THEY want ... you will get more than what YOU want.

Wealthy people build networks, while everyone else looks for work.

Whatever the mind can conceive and believe, the mind can achieve.

It is literally true that you can succeed best and quickest by helping others to succeed.

You can make money or you can make excuses, but you can't make both at the same time.

You must either learn to have self-discipline, or life will discipline you.

Integrity is doing what's right when nobody is looking.

Whatever you expect ... happens.

Doubt is what happens in your heart when vision dies.

By working faithfully eight hours a day, you may eventually get to be boss and work twelve hours a day.

You can lead a horse to water, but you cannot make it drink. But you can *point out why it's thirsty and get it* to *want to drink.*

It amazes me how many people use the same reason to get started as the same excuse to quit. What's even sadder, most of them don't even realize it.

It's not about your resources, it's about your resourcefulness.

Money flows to the leader (as it should).

You don't have to be great to begin ... but you have to begin to become great.

Don't complain about what you have the power to change.

MY DAILY AFFIRMATION

I am building my own financial empire using the only vehicle that enables me to do so — [my network marketing business]. I know by focusing my heart, energy, my passion and my action on recruiting people every day, I am building my dream and I am financially independent and debt free.

I am a leader of people. My work is my ministry, and I am changing thousands of lives. There is no other place where I can have fun, help others, and get rich while doing so. I am the top recruiter in my company today. People are dying to be on my team and they want me to show them how to succeed. I get people to see the recruiting presentation every day. When others reject, they do not reject me, they simply do not understand — and for that I do not blame them. I remain strong and I resolve to help every person to realize that they need to be a part of this crusade. Every person I meet will one day soon be on my team.

I am a champion, a warrior for freedom, an expert recruiter, a winning coach, a caring teammate, and a fearless leader. I am because I say I am, and today I will find the next me!

YOUR DREAM'S FLU SHOT

So that you don't catch the flu from others who have the infection, doctors will give you a small dose/shot of the flu so that your body's immune system can build up resistance to it *before* you come in contact with the virus. Most people say it's worth getting a tiny touch of the flu so that you *don't* catch the full-blown illness.

So, you have just started your network marketing business. Now it's time to inoculate you. When you joined your company, it all seems like such a no-brainer to you. The product is so valuable, needed, and inexpensive. And who wouldn't want to make extra money? Everyone will sign up for this, right? So instead of getting advice and training, you feel it's going to be easy to just pick up the phone and start calling your friends and tell them about it and sign them up.

But guess what ... here's your shot of the flu ... they don't all join! In the beginning, most won't. Some will even try to discourage you. They will say things like:

• I don't need that product • Is that a pyramid scheme? • I don't have time for that • Don't waste your time on that • I know someone who joined and made no money • Nobody makes money in those businesses • Sure, I will come check it out (and they don't show up) • Sure, I will watch the DVD (and they never watch it)

If you understand and expect this from the outset, you can effectively handle these responses and not let it hinder your success. If you have had your flu shot, you can get around people carrying the virus and not become infected yourself. Every top earner in the business got these same responses every day, and *still do*!

Many people claim to be open minded, but in reality most have pre-conceived notions and closed minds. The key is knowing the *right way* to approach people. Coming right out and saying, "Have you heard of [*Company*]?" or "Do you want to make some money?" does *not* work. In fact, running out there without proper training will blow your chance at a good first impression. Of course you are excited and ready to start building your business, but don't sabotage your business on your first day. Learn from the thousands of people who have already made the mistakes before you, and learn what works and what doesn't work. In other words ... STOP! Do not go talk to people yet!

Your friends know you for you, and not as an expert in this new business. They will not take the information properly from you. Don't let your ego convince you otherwise. In your training, you will learn how to utilize your upline experts to share the information properly for you. There are ways to get people in front of the information where they do not feel like their friend is trying to sell/recruit them. The *approach* needs to be right. Then the presentation needs to be third party (PBR/home meeting with expert, PCC/conference call, Business Briefing/seminar at hotel, DVD, or 2-on-1/sit-down meeting with your upline). You will learn this as you attend training events in your area, by listening to the CDs, and listening to weekly team training calls. Your upline experts will also coach you on what to say in your approach to your contacts. Just remember, it's all about *getting appointments*, not explaining anything over the phone or bits and pieces on the fly. *Get appointments* to show them the whole presentation. This is the *only* way you will sign people up. (Maybe by the time you read this, you have already blown it with a few people. Don't keep making the same mistake from here on out.)

So make sure you do not catch the flu (get discouraged and possibly quit when people give you negative responses or objections)! People don't know what they don't know. How can they judge a movie when they *themselves* have never sat in the theater and watched it? They buy into one negative person who has been walking the country infecting everyone with their negative virus. Misery loves company. People love to spread negativity. What you will find is more than half of the people who actually see a whole presentation will sign up! The key is them seeing the whole presentation ... so get appointments! Don't talk to people about it. Be vague and get the presentation in front of them.

Now that you have read this, we hope your baby skin will begin to become rhino skin. Decide to become bullet- proof, and not let words from others knock you out of the box of *your* business. You wouldn't let someone talk you out of your faith, or your family, or your job. So don't let them talk you out of your vehicle that will take you to your dreams and goals. Get good at spotting dream killers and avoid them. Focus on *why* you started this business ... what you want success in this business to accomplish for you. When your *Why* is super strong, so will your resolve to work, grow and succeed. See you at the top!

Customize and Print a copy of this article as a one-page handout for every new person who joins your team at **www.buildinganempirebook.com/flu-shot**

TRIPLE YOUR RECRUITING IN THE NEXT 60 DAYS WITH THE ULTIMATE PROSPECTING TOOL!

Aren't you *TIRED* of trying to convince people that they should look at your business opportunity?

There is a *BETTER WAY*!

The first book I wrote was called *Making My First Ten Million*. This book was written to serve two purposes. The first goal is to help change the reader's mindset and philosophy about money, and to help him/her begin to attract money like never before.

The second purpose for this book is to be used by network marketers as a tool to open the minds of people they would like to introduce to their business model. A common challenge for anyone in the home-based business world is to find people who are open and interested in hearing about their business. By leading with this book, you will be swinging open their mental door of receptivity. Once open, you can walk right in and share your incredible life-changing business to a receptive ear. History and experience show that talking to someone who is not consciously interested in creating wealth will always be met with resistance. In effect, you have likely been trying to share your business through a closed door all of this time!

How would you like to only talk to/meet with people who have a red-hot, burning desire to create a big income? Wouldn't that make your business much more fun? This book represents The Key to the Door of Receptivity. It will be the spark to ignite that burning desire in your audience.

The book has been priced so that it can be given away as your calling card — a card that will resonate and speak to people when you are not there. This book is the seed that you will plant, which will, in turn, create a bountiful harvest. *This is the ultimate prospecting tool!* The book weighs just over an ounce and can be mailed with little postage in a regular envelope. Of course, handing it out may be even better!

And priced at as little as $1 each, the question is how many can your team get into the hands of prospects in the marketplace. Can you imagine 10 people under you getting out just 10 a week? That's 100 warmed-up prospects a week ready to take a look at your business. Or think bigger — have 100 people giving out 100 books a month. With 10,000 opened doors a month to share your business … imagine how fast your business would grow!

STOP trying to jam your opportunity into people's faces only to get a stiff-arm.

START presenting your offer to people who now say, "I'm all ears … show me the best way to build my wealth!"

If you want to triple your recruiting in the next 60 days, get your team handing out these books, and filling their pipeline with *interested* prospects!

To Order Discount Copies:

www.MakingMyFirstTenMillion.com

(see training video on website)

KEEP THE RESOURCES FLOWING ...

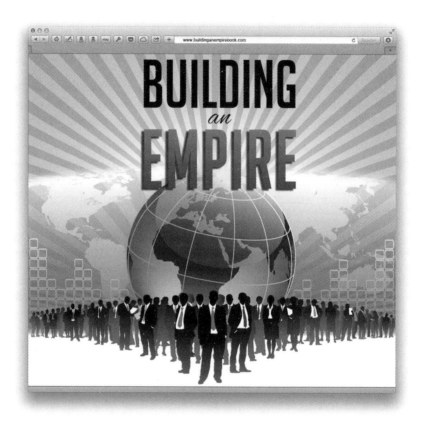

- Additional downloadable resources
- Training videos
- Further tips for building your network marketing business

buildinganempirebook.com

COACHING AT A WHOLE NEW LEVEL

Network marketing cannot be done alone. To become truly successful, you need coaching during all stages of the game.

Let Brian Carruthers become your Foster Mentor. Having built one of the largest organizations in network marketing, Brian can help steer you with motivational tips, proven methods, and even stern warnings as you navigate your way to the top in this industry.

fostermentor.com

ABOUT THE AUTHOR

Prior to becoming the pace-setter for the 300,000+ associates in his network marketing business, Brian enjoyed a successful career in real estate.

A Maryland/DC native, his business knowledge came from many successful associations with very wealthy and successful entrepreneurs — one of whom was his father, who built one of the largest real estate companies on the East Coast in the 1970s.

By the age of 30, Brian pulled all of his experience, knowledge and mentorship and became the mentor for more than 100,000 associates on his team across North America. Brian Carruthers has become a "success coach," helping people to dream again ... then helping them to achieve their dreams. He has already helped thousands of his business associates to become successful business owners, to get out of the corporate world rat-race, and begin to spend real time with their families doing the things that are really important to them.

Brian loves to help people, and gives of himself to that end every day.

"Don't worry about the money," he often says. "Help

enough people get what they want out of life, and you will be taken care of in a big way."

Brian sought out the very best in his field and industry, learned from them, then applied those principles and philosophies to develop the fastest growing and most successful team of entrepreneurs in the U.S.

Brian has been touted by national organizations and business publications as the real deal (see *Home Business* magazine). Becoming such a success by this young age was not just a dream, it was his expectation.

"What you expect, happens," adds Brian. Now his goal is to create thousands of new success stories.

"As our profession grows, and the people in it grow, so will their incomes."